Volume equivalents

IMPERIAL	METRIC	IMPERIAL	METRIC
1fl oz	30ml	15fl oz	450ml
2fl oz	60ml	16fl oz	500ml
2½fl oz	75ml	1 pint	600ml
3½fl oz	100ml	1¼ pints	750ml
4fl oz	120ml	1½ pints	900ml
5fl oz (¼ pint)	150ml	1¾ pints	1 liter
6fl oz	175ml	2 pints	1.2 liters
7fl oz (⅓ pint)	200ml	2½ pints	1.4 liters
8fl oz	240ml	2¾ pints	1.5 liters
10fl oz (½ pint)	300ml	3 pints	1.7 liters
12fl oz	350ml	3½ pints	2 liters
14fl oz	400ml	5¼ pints	3 liters

Weight equivalents

IMPERIAL	METRIC	IMPERIAL	METRIC
½oz	15g	5½oz	150g
¾oz	20g	6oz	175g
scant 1oz	25g	7oz	200g
1oz	30g	8oz	225g
1½oz	45g	9oz	250g
1¾oz	50g	10oz	300g
2oz	60g	1lb	450g
2½oz	75g	1lb 2oz	500g
3oz	85g	1½lb	675g
3½oz	100g	2lb	900g
4oz	115g	2¼lb	1kg
4½oz	125g	3lb 3oz	1.5kg
5oz	140g	4lb	1.8kg

everyday easy

30-minute Dinners

Based on content previously published
in *The Illustrated Kitchen Bible*
and *The Illustrated Quick Cook*

everyday easy
30-minute Dinners

quick assembly • fresh and light • from the pantry

LONDON, NEW YORK, MELBOURNE,
MUNICH, AND DELHI

US Editor
Margaret Parrish

Designer
Elma Aquino

Editorial Assistant
Shashwati Tia Sarkar

Senior Jacket Creative
Nicola Powling

Managing Editors
Dawn Henderson, Angela Wilkes

Managing Art Editor
Christine Keilty

Production Editor
Maria Elia

Production Controller
Hema Gohil

Creative Technical Support
Sonia Charbonnier

DK INDIA

Head of Publishing
Aparna Sharma

Editors
Dipali Singh, Saloni Talwar

Designer
Devika Dwarkadas

DTP Coordinator
Sunil Sharma

DTP Designer
Tarun Sharma

Material first published in *The Illustrated Kitchen Bible*, 2008
and *The Illustrated Quick Cook*, 2009
This edition first published in the United States in 2010
by DK Publishing, 375 Hudson Street
New York, New York 10014

10 11 12 13 14 10 9 8 7 6 5 4 3 2 1
177766—May 2010

Published in Great Britain by Dorling Kindersley Limited.

A catalog record for this book is available
from the Library of Congress.

ISBN 978-0-7566-6189-2

Color reproduction by MDP, Bath
Printed and bound in Singapore by Star Standard

CONTENTS

INTRODUCTION

Fast food that is good food—surely that is the holy grail for all of us? Sometimes it feels like the last thing we have time for is to cook a meal from scratch and it's all too easy to reach for the additive-laden, preprepared meal in the freezer, but preparing delicious, nutritious food doesn't have to be time-consuming. The truth is that oven heating those frozen burgers takes nearly as long as making your own. (Don't believe it? Turn to page 178.)

Many favorite recipes from around the world are often easier, and quicker, to make than they appear. Thailand's famous Pad Thai, Paneer and Peas from India, and the Caribbean classic Rice and Beans can all be made in minutes.

Speedy cooking is made much simpler if you are prepared for those days when you have no time to shop. Having the basics in the house means you can cook up a feast at the shortest notice. The Useful Information section at the start of the book gives invaluable advice on **Stocking Up**: what to keep in your pantry, fridge, and freezer, how to store it, and how to use it.

Next, a selection of step-by-step **Techniques** will refine your core cooking skills and help you save on preparation time, whether you are cooking the perfect pasta or preparing a prickly pineapple. These show you the best quick cooking methods, such as broiling, frying, and steaming—all great choices when you need good food, fast—and ingredients, such as eggs, that are one of the best ingredients a time-strapped cook can have on hand.

Following this is a range of **Recipe Planners** that showcase recipes by themes such as Healthy, One-pot, and Vegetarian so cooks in a hurry can easily find something suitable. For those of you who are particularly short of time, look no further than the Within 15 Minutes section!

Simple dishes using minimal ingredients are the centerpieces in the **Fresh and Light** section. There are great ideas for quick assembly meals, such as the classics Waldorf Salad and Caesar Salad, light dishes that are perfect for summer, such as Vegetable Kebabs and Pea and Mint Soup, and feel-good snacks, such as Stuffed Mushrooms and Scrambled Eggs with Smoked Salmon.

When little fresh food seems to be on hand, turn to your pantry, fridge, freezer, and the **From the Pantry** section for inspiration. A jar of olives, a can of beans, a hunk of cheese, some frozen peas—all can be turned into satisfying meals at lightning speed. Using ingredients you can literally take "from the pantry" and just one or two basic fresh ingredients, such as herbs, you can create tasty dishes such as Pasta with Pecorino and Peas or Bean Burgers.

If you're in the mood for something warming and substantial, choose something from the **Hearty and Filling** section. Chicken Fajitas with Tomato and Avocado Salsa and Lamb Koftas are great weeknight fare that you can eat with your fingers, while Cauliflower Cheese and Sweet and Sour Stir-fried Fish with Ginger are guaranteed to be hits with the family.

At the end of a meal, there's no need to spend a lot of effort on the dessert when there are ingenious ideas in the **Quick Desserts** section that deliver instant gratification. Try the Banoffee Pie or Citrus Fruit Salad for sweet treats that need no cooking, while Knickerbocker Glory and Eton Mess are timeless favorites that are sure to be eaten with relish by young and old alike.

The secret of the quickest recipes is to keep things simple. A handful of good ingredients and a stock of good recipes are all you need. It's so easy anyone can do it—day in, day out.

Stocking up

All you need is a well-stocked pantry and refrigerator to form the basis of a good meal. When you don't have time to shop, you will always have something around to make a quick supper.

SPICES, HERBS

Paprika is best for pork and chicken dishes. Store for 6 months.
Ground coriander and seeds are best for Indian-style dishes. Store for 6 months.
Ground chili and chili flakes are best for adding spice and heat to Indian, Thai, and Mediterranean dishes. Store for 6 months.
Ground cumin and seeds can be added to a soup, stew, or marinade. Store for 6 months.
Ground cinnamon and sticks are best for chicken and lamb stews. Store for 6 months.
Curry powder is best for chicken, lamb, and beef. Store for 6 months.
Dried herbs such as oregano, thyme, mixed dried herbs, and bay leaves are best for chicken, lamb, and fish dishes, stews, and casseroles. Store for 6 months.

PASTA, RICE, NOODLES

Pasta, in its many shapes and sizes, makes a quick and easy supper and is best for sauces and bakes. Store for 1 year.
Rice is available in many varieties—basmati, brown, long grain, risotto (arborio or carnaroli), and paella. It is best used in pilaf and salads, and for serving as an accompaniment to meat and fish. Store for 6 months.
Noodles are available in a selection of types and thicknesses. You can choose from egg, rice, wheat, and buckwheat noodles. You can even buy straight-to-wok noodles, which require no cooking, just heating through. Best for Asian-style dishes, soups, salads, or stir-fries. Store for 6 months.

LEGUMES, GRAINS, NUTS, FRUITS

Legumes include canned and dried Puy lentils, red lentils, green lentils, and yellow split peas. Canned and dried chickpeas, kidney beans, and butter or lima beans are always useful. Best for stews, salads, bakes, casseroles, dips, and soups. Store for 1 year.
Grains such as farro, pearl barley, couscous, bulgur wheat, and polenta are best for salads and hot pots. Store for 1 year.
Nuts and seeds include a selection of whole peanuts, walnuts, and cashew nuts, chopped and ground almonds; sesame seeds, sunflower seeds, and pumpkin seeds. They are best for toppings, in salads, and stir-fries. Store for 6 months.
Dried fruit such as raisins, cranberries, dates, figs, and apricots can be used in salads and stews. Store for 6 months.

OILS, CONDIMENTS, SAUCES

Oils include olive, sunflower, groundnut, and sesame oil, and are best for dressings, salads, marinades, stir-fries, pan frying, and baking. Store for 6 months.
Vinegars such as red wine, white wine, rice wine, balsamic, and sherry vinegar are best for salads, dressings, and marinades. Store for 1 year.
Mustards such as English, Dijon, and wholegrain add flavor to dishes and dressings. Store for 1 year.
Pesto and pastes include harissa, tomato paste, and Thai curry paste and are best for curry dishes, stirring into casseroles, or for adding to pasta. Store for 6 months.
Sauces such as soy sauce, fish sauce, Worcestershire sauce, and oyster sauce are best for stir-fries, stews, and casseroles. Store for 1 year.

JARS, CANS, POWDERS

Black and green olives, and small salted **capers** are best for pasta, salads, and dips. Store for 1 year.
Canned whole or chopped tomatoes and sun-dried tomatoes can be added to stews, casseroles, and pasta sauces. Store for 1 year.
Sweetcorn is best for soups or stews. Store for 1 year.
Tuna and salmon can be stored canned, and are best for pasta, salads, fish cakes, and bakes. Store for 1 year.
Anchovies can be stored in jars or canned in olive oil or salt. They are best for pasta, salads, casseroles, and stews. Store for 1 year.
Coconut milk is best for Thai curries. Store for 1 year.
Powdered stock (bouillon) is available in chicken, beef, and vegetable form and is best for gravies, sauces, soups, and stews. Store for 1 year.

DAIRY FOODS, EGGS

Milk is best for sauces, batters, and desserts. Whole milk gives the best flavor, but low-fat is the most popular, since it contains far less fat content than whole. Skim is best reserved for drinks. Store for 7 days (or until the use-by date), or freeze for 1 month.
Butter and cheese enrich all hot dishes and cheese adds instant protein to a quick dish. Available in different varieties, they are best for sauces, bakes, baking, and sandwiches. Store for 1 month (or until the use-by date), or freeze for up to 3 months.
Eggs are best kept in the refrigerator, unless you plan to use them within a couple of days of purchase. Use them for omelets, salads, and sandwiches. Store for 3 weeks (or until the use-by date).

FREEZER FOODS

Vegetables can be bought frozen, but peas and fava beans are the only vegetables that withstand the freezing process without it impairing their flavor. They make a great standby and are best for instant soups. You can even add them to fish or meat pies, casseroles, or as a meal accompaniment. Store for 6 months.
Meat freezes well in the form of ground beef, lamb, or pork sausages; use for chilli, ragù, hot dogs, and sandwiches. Store for 6 months. Freeze raw meat and poultry for up to 3 months.
Fish and seafood include fish fillets (such as haddock, pollack, and salmon) and shrimp (shell on or off). They are best for fish pies, stir-fries, and barbecues. Store for 3 months.

A guide to symbols

The recipes in this book are accompanied by symbols that alert you to important information.

Tells you how many people the recipe serves, or how much is produced.

Indicates how much time you will need to prepare and cook a dish. Next to this symbol you will also find out if additional time is required for such things as marinating, standing, or cooling. Read the recipe to find out exactly how much extra time to allow.

Points out a healthy dish—low in fat or low GI (Glycemic Index).

This is especially important, since it alerts you to what has to be done before you can begin to cook the recipe, or to parts of the recipe that may take a long time to complete.

This denotes that special equipment is required, such as a deep-fat fryer or skewers. Where possible, alternatives are given.

This symbol accompanies freezing information.

TECHNIQUES

Grill or Broil

Fish, vegetables, and tender, prime cuts of meat (demonstrated here) are suitable for cooking under the broiler, on a barbecue, or on a ridged cast-iron grill pan.

1 Heat the grill pan over high heat until very hot. Prepare the meat by brushing both sides with oil, using a pastry brush. Season with a little salt and pepper.

2 Cook the meat for 1 minute, then rotate it 45 degrees to achieve crossing grill marks and cook for another 1–2 minutes. Repeat on the other side. Remove and allow to rest before serving.

Pan-fry

This quick cooking method is best suited to lean cuts of meat, fish (demonstrated here), or tender vegetables. Use a shallow frying pan and a little oil or fat.

1 Season the fish with salt and pepper. Heat 1/2 tbsp olive oil or sunflower oil in a nonstick frying pan until hot (but not spitting). Add the fish, and leave to cook for 2–3 minutes.

2 Turn the fish over, and cook the other side for 2–3 minutes, or longer if the fish fillet is thick. Keep the heat at medium-high. Turn the fish over again (it should be an even golden color), and serve.

Stir-fry

Stir-frying can be used to cook meat, fish, and vegetables (demonstrated here). Chop your ingredients to the same size, keep the heat high, and stir constantly.

1 Heat the wok or large frying pan over a medium-high heat, then add 1/2 tbsp vegetable or sunflower oil. Heat until hot and sizzling. Add any spices first, and stir-fry vigorously for a minute.

2 Add the vegetables in order of firmness (firmest first). Continue stirring so the vegetables don't burn. Stir-fry for 4–5 minutes until the vegetables are cooked. Season well and serve.

Steam

Steaming is a healthy way to cook vegetables, meat, and fish (demonstrated here), and ensures that none of the flavors are lost during cooking.

1 To use a bamboo steamer, pour water into a wok to just below where the steamer fits. Add any flavorings, then bring to a simmer. Put the basket in the wok, but ensure the base is above the water.

2 Steam the fish with any extra flavorings until opaque and flaking easily. Allow 3–4 minutes for fillets, 6–8 minutes for fish up to 12oz (350g), and 12–15 minutes for fish up to 2lb (900g).

Soak and cook rice

To cook perfect rice, use $1^1/_2$ times as much water or stock as rice. Always be sure to soak and rinse the rice before cooking.

Put rice and liquid into a large saucepan. Over medium heat, bring to a boil, stir once, and lower the heat to simmer the rice, uncovered, for 10–12 minutes, or until all the liquid is absorbed. Remove from the heat and cover with a clean, folded dish towel and a fitted lid on top of that. Leave the rice to steam, without removing the lid, for 20 minutes. Remove the folded dish towel and replace the lid. Leave the rice to sit for 5 minutes, covered. Fluff the rice with a fork and serve.

Boil noodles

While rice noodles only need to be soaked in hot water before use, other noodles need to be boiled. Rinsing under cold water refreshes them.

1 To boil egg, wheat, or buckwheat noodles, bring a large saucepan of water to a boil. Add the noodles, return to a boil, then cook until the noodles are softened and flexible—about 2 minutes.

2 Drain the noodles in a colander and place them under cold running water. Toss the noodles with a little oil to prevent them from sticking, then serve or proceed with the desired recipe.

Cook dried pasta

Dried pasta is essential to have in your pantry, since it can form the basis of many quick dishes, but it's all too easy to overcook it.

1 Bring a large pan of salted water to a boil; gently pour in the pasta. Boil uncovered, following the recommended cooking time on the package, or until *al dente* (cooked, but firm to the bite) when tasted.

2 As soon as the pasta is *al dente*, quickly drain it through a colander, shaking it gently to remove any excess water. Toss the pasta with a little oil, then serve or proceed with the recipe.

Make couscous

With no cooking on the burner or in the oven, couscous is quick and easy to prepare. Use around $1^3/_4$ times as much water as couscous.

1 Pour the quick-cook couscous and a pinch of salt into a large bowl and pour over boiling water. Cover with a folded dish towel, leave for 5 minutes, remove the dish towel, and fluff up with a fork.

2 Re-cover the bowl and leave for another 5 minutes. Remove the dish towel and add either 1 tbsp olive oil or a pat of unsalted butter and fluff up the couscous again until light. Serve.

Test eggs for freshness

In addition to checking the best-before date on the egg carton, you can use this simple test to check how fresh your eggs are: immerse the egg in water and see if it rises. A stale egg contains much more air and less liquid than a fresh one, so it will float. Do not use a stale egg.

Fresh

Borderline

Stale

Boil eggs

Despite the name, eggs must be simmered—never boiled. If a green ring appears, it is the result of overcooking (or an old egg).

For soft-boiled

The whites are set and the yolks runny. In a deep pan, cover the eggs with cold water and bring to a boil. Lower to a simmer for 2–3 minutes.

For hard-boiled

Both the whites and yolks are set. Simmer for 10 minutes from a boil. Place the pan under cold running water to stop cooking; peel when cool.

Scramble eggs

Scramble as you like, whether you prefer your curds large or small. Before you begin, beat the eggs in a bowl, and season with salt and pepper.

1 Heat a nonstick pan over medium heat, then melt a pat of butter to coat the bottom lightly. When the butter has melted, but not yet browned, pour in the beaten eggs.

2 Using a wooden spoon, pull the setting egg from the edges of the pan into the center to cook the raw egg. For larger curds, let the egg set longer before scrambling.

Make an omelet

A 3-egg omelet is the easiest to handle; any more than 6 eggs is difficult. Before you begin, beat the eggs in a bowl, and season with salt and pepper.

1 Heat a nonstick frying pan over medium heat and melt a pat of butter. Add the eggs, tilting the pan so the eggs can spread evenly. Stir the eggs with a fork to distribute the eggs evenly.

2 Stop stirring the eggs as soon as they are set. Fold the side of the omelet nearest to you halfway over itself. Flip it halfway over again, then slide it on to a plate, and serve immediately.

Segment citrus fruit

Preparing citrus fruit this way ensures clean and precise wedges for a more attractive garnish.

1 Cut the ends off the fruit so it stands upright. Holding it firmly, slice along the contour of the skin, removing as much of the pith as possible.

2 Slice along the lines of the membrane that separates each slice. Repeat slicing between each membrane until the fruit is fully segmented.

Prepare mango

Cutting into halves along the fibrous pit and "hedgehogging" the mango is the cleanest way to remove the flesh.

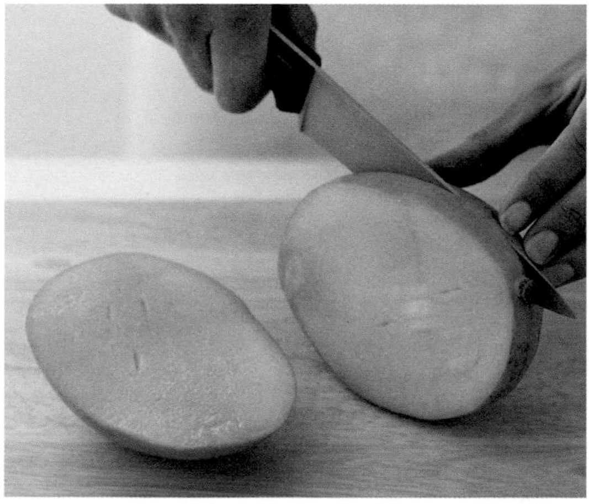

1 Stand the mango on its side and cut it just to one side of the pit; repeat on the other side to make 2 halves. A slice containing the pit will remain.

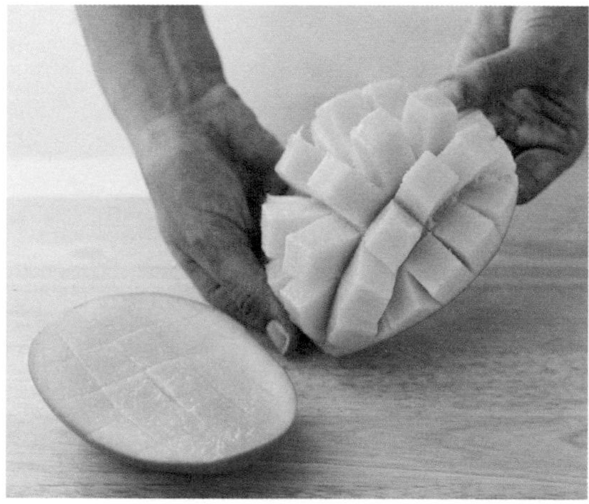

2 Cut the flesh into square segments, cutting to, but not through, the skin. Invert the skin to expose the flesh. Cut along the skin to remove the flesh.

Prepare pineapple

Take care when handling the sharp outer skin and use the sharpest knife you can find, since the inner core is tough.

1 Slice both ends off the pineapple. Stand it on its base, and slice the skin from the top down, all the way around the fruit.

2 Cut it in half lengthwise, then into wedges, and slice away the fibrous core that runs through the center of the fruit.

Prepare pomegranate

This delicious Middle Eastern fruit has a tough skin and requires patience when preparing, but it's worth the effort.

1 Slice the fruit into quarters, using a sharp knife. The juicy, red seeds are clustered and divided by thin, pithy membranes that are bitter in taste.

2 Over a bowl, gently invert each quarter to make the seeds come loose. Pick out any seeds that remain. Remove any membranes and discard.

Healthy

Bean burgers page 114

Baked white fish in wine and herbs page 72

Leaf-wrapped Asian sole page 42

Thai-style minced pork page 186

Lentil, fava bean, and feta salad page 88

Sweet and sour stir-fried fish with ginger page 168

Classic Chinese wontons page 70

Pea and mint soup page 80

Vegetarian Pad Thai page 90

Hot and sour beef stir-fry with green beans page 188

Tuna and white beans with olives page 104

Vietnamese salad of broiled shrimp with papaya page 44

One-pot

Seared duck with five-spice and noodles page 180

Rice and black-eyed peas page 122

Linguine with tomato clam sauce page 92

Kidneys with mustard sauce page 134

Orechiette with pancetta page 56

Pasta with mushroom sauce page 172

Pasta with Pecorino and peas page 106

Mussels in fennel broth page 140

Vegetarian Pad Thai page 90

Kasha pilaf page 84

Lamb with blueberries page 136

Spiced orzo with spinach page 82

Minced chicken with exotic mushooms, soy, and lime page 146

Spaetzle page 98

Vegetarian

Cauliflower cheese page 174

Vegetable kebabs page 76

Egg noodles with lemon grass and herbs page 78

Waldorf salad page 52

Spaetzle page 98

Rice and black-eyed peas page 122

Gnocchi with Gorgonzola and walnut sauce page 110

Fettucine Alfredo page 94

Paneer and peas page 116

Pasta with olives, capers, and sun-dried tomatoes page 118

Kasha pilaf page 84

Asparagus, broccoli, ginger, and mint stir-fry page 150

Grated zucchini and goat cheese omelet page 66

Stuffed mushrooms page 36

Tomato and harissa tart page 156

Spiced orzo with spinach page 82

Cold

Lentils with artichokes and peppers page 108

Couscous with pine nuts and almonds page 74

Tuna and white beans with olives page 104

Waldorf salad page 52

Crab salad page 48

Layered marinated herring salad page 34

Tomato bulgur wheat with capers and olives page 100

Pea and mint soup page 80

Lobster salad with watercress page 60

Lentil, fava bean, and feta salad page 88

Bulgur with mixed peppers, mint, and paprika page 148

Caesar salad page 46

Budget

Rice balls filled with cheese page 96

Turkey burgers page 182

Caesar salad page 46

Boudin noir and sautéed apples page 142

Egg fu yung page 112

Simple cheese omelet page 40

Danish meatballs page 130

Egg and fennel potato salad page 170

Waldorf salad page 52

Welsh rarebit page 120

Pork scallops page 184

Hamburgers page 178

Within 15 minutes—Savory

Egg noodles with lemon grass and herbs page 78

Grilled halibut with green sauce page 54

Crab salad page 48

Couscous with pine nuts and almonds page 74

Caesar salad page 46

Simple cheese omelet page 40

Lentils with artichokes and peppers page 108

Within 15 minutes—Sweet

Banoffee pie page 220

Pear and grape salad page 214

Zabaglione page 192

Knickerbocker glory page 218

Pear gratin page 210

Warm fruit compote page 198

Eton mess page 194

FRESH AND LIGHT

Layered marinated herring salad

For convenience and speedy cooking, buy marinated herring fillets at the supermarket.

INGREDIENTS

1 sweet onion, thinly sliced
1 cup sour cream
1/2 cup plain yogurt
1 tbsp fresh lemon juice
1/4 tsp sugar
2 tart apples, such as Granny Smith, peeled, cored, and thinly sliced
2 small sour pickles (cornichons), chopped
salt and freshly ground black pepper
10oz (300g) marinated herring fillets, drained
2 cooked potatoes, sliced (optional)
1 small cooked beet, peeled, if necessary, and diced (optional)
1 tbsp chopped dill, to garnish

METHOD

1 Soak the onion in a bowl of cold water for 15 minutes. Drain well, then toss with the sour cream, yogurt, lemon juice, and sugar. Stir in the apples and pickles, and season with salt and pepper.

2 Place half the herring in a serving dish and top with the potatoes and beets, if using. Cover with half the sour cream mixture. Layer the remaining herring, potatoes, and beets on top, then spread with the remaining sauce.

3 Cover the dish tightly with plastic wrap and refrigerate. Sprinkle with dill just before serving.

GOOD WITH Chunks of sourdough bread or slices of pumpernickel.

PREPARE AHEAD The salad can be assembled up to 2 days in advance and chilled until required.

6–10 servings

prep 15 mins, plus soaking and chilling

Stuffed mushrooms

Portobello mushrooms, or those with open cups, make great bases for fillings.

INGREDIENTS

8 portobello mushrooms
2 tbsp olive oil, plus more for greasing
4 shallots, finely chopped
2 garlic cloves, minced
3/4 cup pine nuts, toasted
1/4 cup roughly torn basil
1/4 cup finely chopped parsley
salt and freshly ground black pepper
6oz (175g) firm goat cheese, cut into 8 slices
8 slices pancetta, unrolled into strips

METHOD

1 Preheat the oven to 375°F (190°C). Place the mushrooms on a lightly oiled baking sheet.

2 Heat the oil in a large frying pan over medium heat. Add the shallots and cook for 2 minutes, stirring frequently, until softened. Add the garlic and cook for 1 minute. Stir in the pine nuts, basil, and parsley and season with salt and pepper.

3 Spoon the mixture into the mushrooms. Top each with a slice of goat cheese. Wrap a pancetta strip around each mushroom, tucking the ends underneath.

4 Bake for 15–20 minutes, or until the mushrooms are tender and the pancetta is crisp. Serve immediately.

GOOD WITH A mixed green salad and a drizzle of balsamic vinegar.

4 servings

prep 10 mins
• cook 20 mins

Scrambled eggs with smoked salmon

This feel-good recipe is great at any time of the day.

INGREDIENTS

6 large eggs
2 tbsp whole milk
salt and freshly ground black pepper
1 tbsp butter
8oz (225g) smoked salmon, cut into thin strips, or hot smoked salmon, flaked
2 tbsp finely chopped chives
4 English muffins, split and toasted

METHOD

1 Beat the eggs with the milk, and season with salt and pepper.

2 Heat the butter in a medium nonstick frying pan over medium heat until foaming. Add the eggs and stir with a wooden spoon until almost set. Stir in the smoked salmon and cook until just set.

3 Sprinkle with the chives. Spoon over the toasted muffin halves and serve hot.

4 servings

prep 15 mins • cook 3 mins

Simple cheese omelet

A great omelet is cooked only just to the point of being "done"; a sprinkle of cheese is the perfect finishing touch.

INGREDIENTS

2 eggs
drop of milk
salt and freshly ground black pepper
1 tbsp butter
handful of grated cheese

METHOD

1 Crack the eggs into a bowl and lightly whisk with a drop of milk. Season with salt and pepper.

2 Heat a small frying pan over a medium heat until hot, then add the butter. Once the butter is melted and foaming, pour in the egg mixture. Pull the edges away from the side of the pan using a spatula or fork; keep doing this so that any uncooked mixture runs to the edge. After about 30 seconds, most of the egg should be set. It will still be soft in the middle, but residual heat will continue cooking the omelet after it is taken out of the pan.

3 Sprinkle the cheese down the center of the omelet, then fold one half of the omelet over the top of the other. Slide on to a plate, and serve immediately.

GOOD WITH A fresh, mixed leaf salad.

Leaf-wrapped Asian sole

Gently steamed fish makes a healthy, tasty supper.

INGREDIENTS

4 sole fillets, about 6oz (175g) each
4 tsp fresh lemon juice
4 tsp soy sauce
2 tsp fresh ginger, peeled and grated
Asian sesame oil, for drizzling
1/4 tsp ground white pepper
16–20 large bok choy leaves, tough stalks removed

METHOD

1 Drizzle each sole fillet with 1 tsp lemon juice, 1 tsp soy sauce, 1/2 tsp ginger, and a light, even drizzle of sesame oil. Season with white pepper. Gently roll the fillets lengthwise and arrange them on a heat-proof plate.

2 Fill a large saucepan equipped with a steamer with 1in (2.5cm) water; bring to a boil, then reduce the heat to a simmer.

3 Blanch the bok choy leaves for several seconds in the water, or until soft, then place them briefly into a bowl of iced water.

4 Wrap each fillet in 4–5 leaves, securing with toothpicks if necessary. Set the plate with the fish on the steamer rack, place the lid on the steamer, and steam for 8–10 minutes, or until the fish becomes opaque.

GOOD WITH A mix of stir-fried vegetables, or with boiled white rice.

4 servings

prep 15 mins
• cook 10 mins

healthy option

large saucepan equipped with a steamer rack
• toothpicks

Vietnamese salad of broiled shrimp with papaya

Vietnamese cuisine is noted for its fresh, clean flavors: lime, mint, chilis, and fish sauce are all widely used.

INGREDIENTS

12 large shrimp, peeled and deveined
2 tbsp Asian fish sauce
1 tbsp fresh lime juice
1 tsp rice wine vinegar
1 tsp sugar
1 small fresh hot red chili, seeded and minced
2 garlic cloves, minced into a paste
1 green papaya, peeled, seeded, quartered lengthwise, and cut into julienne strips
½ cucumber, peeled, seeded, and cut into julienne strips
1 tbsp chopped mint, plus sprigs to garnish

METHOD

1 Position a broiler rack 4in (10cm) from the source of heat. Preheat the broiler. Line the rack with aluminum foil and lightly oil. Spread the shrimp on the foil and brush with oil. Broil for 2–3 minutes, turning once, until the shrimp turn opaque.

2 Meanwhile, whisk the fish sauce, lime juice, vinegar, sugar, chili, garlic, and 6 tbsp cold water together in a bowl until the sugar dissolves. Add the shrimp to the bowl and stir. Let stand until cooled.

3 Add the papaya, cucumber, and chopped mint, and toss together. Transfer the salad to a serving platter, and arrange the shrimp on top. Garnish with the mint sprigs and serve at once.

PREPARE AHEAD Steps 1 and 2 can be completed several hours in advance and stored, covered, in the refrigerator.

Caesar salad

Anchovies help to give this classic salad its traditional flavor, but they can be omitted from the dressing, if preferred.

INGREDIENTS

For the dressing

2 garlic cloves, diced into a purée
2 anchovy fillets in olive oil, drained and finely chopped
½ cup extra-virgin olive oil
2 tbsp fresh lemon juice
1 tsp Worcestershire sauce
freshly ground black pepper

2 small heads of romaine lettuce
1 cup croûtons
2 large eggs
½ cup Parmesan cheese, shaved or grated

METHOD

1 To make the dressing, mash the garlic and anchovies together to make a thick paste. Scrape into a screw-top jar, add the olive oil, lemon juice, Worcestershire sauce, and pepper to taste. Shake until well blended and thick. Set aside.

2 To assemble the salad, tear the lettuce into bite-sized pieces and toss with the croûtons in a salad bowl. Bring a small saucepan of water to a boil over high heat. Reduce the heat to medium, add the eggs, and boil gently for 2 minutes, no longer. Drain and rinse well in cold water.

3 Crack open the eggs, scoop over the lettuce, and toss. Shake the dressing well, pour over the salad, and toss again. Sprinkle with the Parmesan cheese and serve at once.

GOOD WITH All barbecued meats. It is especially good served with chunks of French bread.

PREPARE AHEAD The dressing can be made in advance; keep chilled in an airtight container for up to 1 week.

Crab salad with mango dressing

This tasty summer dish proves how well crab matches with fruit.

INGREDIENTS

For the dressing

1 ripe mango, peeled, pitted, and diced
3 tbsp olive oil
zest and juice of 1/2 lime

1 shallot, finely chopped
2 tbsp chopped cilantro
1 tbsp chopped mint leaves
5oz (140g) mixed salad greens
1lb (450g) fresh crabmeat, picked over
1 ripe avocado, peeled, pitted, and sliced lengthwise

METHOD

1 To make the dressing, purée the mango, oil, lime zest, and juice in a food processor or blender. Season with salt and pepper, adding a little water, if too thick.

2 Toss the shallot, cilantro, and mint with the salad greens in a large bowl. Add a few spoonfuls of dressing and toss again. Divide among 4 plates and top each with equal amounts of crab and avocado. Serve at once, passing the rest of the dressing on the side.

GOOD WITH Slices of freshly baked Irish soda bread.

4 servings

prep 15 mins

purchase the crab on the day you intend to make the salad

food processor

Chicken poached in coconut milk

Give chicken a fragrant flavor by cooking it in this rich broth.

INGREDIENTS

8 boneless chicken breast halves (preferably free-range), skin on, about 7oz (200g) each
2 cups hot chicken or vegetable stock
one 14oz (400ml) can unsweetened coconut milk, well shaken to blend
3 bay leaves
3 garlic cloves, peeled but left whole
salt and freshly ground black pepper

METHOD

1 To poach the chicken, put the breasts in a large pan over medium heat, then pour in the hot stock and the coconut milk. Add the bay leaves and garlic cloves, and season with salt and pepper. Bring to a boil, then cover the pan, reduce the heat to low, and simmer for 10–15 minutes until the chicken is cooked through. Poke a sharp knife into the flesh to check—the juices should run clear.

2 Using a slotted spoon, remove the chicken from the pan, and leave to cool for a minute or two. When cool enough to handle, discard the skin and either slice or shred the chicken using two forks, and serve with a little of the coconut poaching liquid.

GOOD WITH Any rice, but especially boiled basmati rice.

Waldorf salad

A classic salad named after the prestigious Waldorf-Astoria Hotel in New York City.

INGREDIENTS

1lb (450g) crisp, red-skinned apples, cored and diced
2 tbsp fresh lemon juice
4 celery stalks, sliced
1/2 cup mayonnaise
salt and freshly ground black pepper
2/3 cup walnuts, toasted and coarsely chopped

METHOD

1 Toss the diced apples and lemon juice well in a medium bowl.

2 Add the celery and mayonnaise, and mix. Season with salt and pepper. Cover with plastic wrap and refrigerate.

3 Stir in the walnuts. Transfer to a serving dish and serve well chilled.

4 servings

prep 20 mins, plus chilling

Grilled halibut with green sauce

A fresh-tasting dish that is easy to prepare and cooks in minutes.

INGREDIENTS

For the green sauce

1 cup packed mixed herbs
(parsley, chives, mint, tarragon, and chervil)
½ cup olive oil
1 tbsp tarragon vinegar
2 garlic cloves
salt and freshly ground black pepper
sugar (optional)

6 thick halibut fillets, about 5oz (140g) each
1 tbsp olive oil
salt and freshly ground black pepper
lemon wedges, for serving

METHOD

1 Process the herbs, oil, tarragon vinegar, and garlic in a blender until smooth. Season with salt and pepper. If it tastes slightly bitter, add sugar to taste. Transfer the sauce to a bowl, cover, and refrigerate until serving.

2 Preheat the broiler or build a fire in an outdoor grill. Lightly brush each fillet with oil and season with salt and pepper. Broil or grill, turning once, about 4 minutes, until the fish is barely opaque when pierced with the tip of a sharp knife. Transfer to plates and serve, with the green sauce and the lemon wedges.

Orecchiette with pancetta

Short pastas such as orecchiette (literally, "little ears" in Italian) work well with oil-based dressings.

INGREDIENTS

1lb (450g) dried orecchiette pasta
2 tbsp olive oil
6oz (175g) pancetta, chopped
2 zucchini, diced
3 garlic cloves, chopped
1/2 crushed hot red pepper
1 cup thawed frozen peas
6 tbsp freshly grated Parmesan
3 tbsp chopped parsley
salt and freshly ground black pepper

METHOD

1 Cook the orecchiette in a large pot of lightly salted boiling water according to the package instructions, until *al dente*.

2 Meanwhile, heat the oil in a large frying pan over medium heat. Add the pancetta and cook for 5 minutes until lightly golden. Add the zucchini, garlic, and hot pepper and cook for 3 minutes, until the zucchini is crisp-tender. Stir in the peas and cook about 2 minutes.

3 Drain the pasta and return to its pot. Add the pancetta mixture and stir over low heat until combined. Off the heat, stir in the Parmesan and parsley, and season with salt and pepper.

Salad Niçoise

This famous French classic salad is suitable for a main course.

INGREDIENTS

9oz (250g) green beans, trimmed
4 tuna steaks, 5oz (140g) each
3/4 cup extra-virgin olive oil
salt and freshly ground pepper
3 tbsp white wine vinegar
1 1/2 tbsp fresh lemon juice
2 tsp Dijon mustard
1 garlic clove, finely chopped
2 romaine lettuce hearts, trimmed and torn into bite-sized pieces
8–10 basil leaves
9oz (250g) plum tomatoes, quartered lengthwise
12 Kalamata olives
8 anchovy fillets in olive oil, drained
1 small red onion, finely sliced
4 large, hard-boiled eggs, peeled and quartered

METHOD

1 Cook the green beans in gently boiling water, for 3–4 minutes, or until crisp-tender. Drain the beans, rinse well under cold water, and pat dry with paper towels.

2 Heat a ridged grill pan over medium-high heat. Brush the tuna steaks with 1 tbsp olive oil and season with salt and pepper. Sear the tuna for 2 minutes on each side; the centers should be slightly pink.

3 To make the vinaigrette, whisk together the vinegar, lemon juice, mustard, and garlic. Slowly whisk in the remaining olive oil. Season with salt and pepper.

4 Combine the lettuce, basil, green beans, tomatoes, olives, anchovies, and onion in a large bowl. Drizzle with the vinaigrette and toss gently.

5 Divide the salad among 4 plates. Cut each tuna steak in half crosswise and arrange both halves on top of the salad. Garnish with the eggs.

4 servings

prep 25 mins
• cook 8 mins

ridged grill pan

Lobster salad with watercress

A very special summer salad with an interesting mix of flavors.

INGREDIENTS

½ red onion, very thinly sliced
1 tsp red wine vinegar
4 cooked lobster tails
1 large bunch of watercress, tough stalks removed
½ fennel bulb, very thinly sliced
8 sun-dried tomatoes in oil, drained and chopped
chervil, dill, or chives, to garnish

For the dressing

1 large egg
1 large egg yolk
2 tsp Dijon mustard
zest and juice of 1 lemon
1¾ cups vegetable oil
3 tbsp chopped dill and/or chives
salt and freshly ground black pepper

METHOD

1 To make the dressing, combine the egg, egg yolk, mustard, and lemon zest and juice in a food processor. Slowly add the oil. Add the dill and season. Transfer to a bowl, cover, and refrigerate.

2 Combine the red onion and vinegar in a bowl. Let stand for 10 minutes. Drain well.

3 Remove the lobster meat from the shell, and chop it in large chunks.

4 Divide the watercress among 4 plates, and add the fennel, onion, tomatoes, and lobster; drizzle with the dressing. Serve with more dressing served on the side.

Mixed fried fish

Crisp strips of fried fish are served with a peppery mayonnaise sauce.

INGREDIENTS

For the sauce

1 cup packed arugula leaves
½ cup mayonnaise
1 garlic clove, minced
1 tsp fresh lemon juice
salt and freshly ground black pepper

½ cup all-purpose flour
salt and freshly ground black pepper
2 large eggs, beaten
1 cup panko (Japanese bread crumbs)
9oz (250g) mixed skinless white fish fillets, such as cod and snapper
8oz (225g) skinless salmon fillet
12 large shrimp, peeled and deveined
vegetable oil, for deep frying

METHOD

1 To make the sauce, process the arugula, mayonnaise, garlic, and lemon juice until the arugula is puréed. Season with salt and pepper. Spoon into a serving dish and chill until it is time to serve.

2 Place the flour in a shallow bowl and season with salt and pepper. Beat the eggs in a second bowl. Spread the panko in a third bowl. Cut the fish fillets into 8 equal portions. Toss the fish and shrimp in flour, then dip in beaten egg, and coat in panko.

3 Preheat the oven to 200°F (95°C). Pour enough oil into a large, deep saucepan to come halfway up the sides. Heat over high heat to 350°F (180°C). In batches, fry the seafood for 2–3 minutes, or until crisp and golden. Using a slotted spoon, transfer to paper towel-lined baking sheets and keep warm in the oven until all of the fish is fried.

4 Divide the fish among dinner plates and serve immediately, with the sauce served separately.

4 servings

prep 20 mins • cook 10 mins

food processor

Linguine with scallops

Succulent scallops with a hint of chili and lime—perfect for entertaining.

INGREDIENTS

1lb (450g) dried linguine
2 limes
$\frac{1}{3}$ cup olive oil, plus extra for brushing
salt and freshly ground black pepper
1 fresh, hot red chili, seeds removed, and finely chopped
12 large sea scallops
3 tbsp chopped cilantro

METHOD

1 Cook the linguine in boiling, salted water according to package directions, or until *al dente*. Drain and keep warm.

2 While the pasta is cooking, grate the zest and squeeze the juice from 1 of the limes. Whisk the lime juice and olive oil together in a small bowl. Stir in the chili, and half of the cilantro. Season with salt and pepper. Toss the lime mixture with the linguine.

3 Heat a large, heavy frying pan, or ridged grill pan over high heat. Brush the scallops with olive oil, and season with salt and pepper. Add to the pan, and sear the scallops for 3 minutes, turning once.

4 Divide the linguine between 4 serving plates and arrange the scallops on top. Cut the remaining lime into wedges. Serve immediately, with lime wedges.

GOOD WITH Crusty bread and a side salad of arugula with shavings of Parmesan.

PREPARE AHEAD The dressing in step 2 can be made an hour ahead.

4 servings

prep 10 mins
• cook 10 mins

Grated zucchini and goat cheese omelet

Soft goat cheese has a herbaceous character that works well with green vegetables.

INGREDIENTS

3 large eggs, lightly beaten
1 small zucchini, coarsely grated
1 tbsp butter
$^{1}/_{2}$ cup crumbled soft goat cheese
salt and freshly ground black pepper
small handful of thyme sprigs, leaves only, for garnish (optional)

METHOD

1 Combine the egg and zucchini in a bowl. Season with salt and pepper.

2 Melt the butter in a small nonstick frying pan over medium-high heat until foaming, then pour in the egg mixture, swirling it around to the edges of the pan. Gently slide a knife or heat-proof spatula around the edge of the pan to lift the edges of the omelet.

3 When the edges have begun to cook, scatter the goat cheese evenly over the entire surface. Continue cooking until the egg mixture in the center is almost set, but still soft. Remove from the heat, and leave for a minute or two—the retained heat will continue to cook the egg.

4 Season with pepper and garnish with thyme leaves. Carefully fold the omelet into thirds or in half, and slide it out of the pan onto a plate. Serve immediately.

1 serving

prep 10 mins
• cook 15 mins

Lemon-soy skewered chicken with hot dipping sauce

This soy-based marinade doesn't need much time to give the chicken a fresh, tangy flavor.

INGREDIENTS

1 stalk lemon grass, tough outer leaves removed, finely chopped
juice of 1 lemon
1 tbsp soy sauce
1 tsp granulated sugar
salt and freshly ground black pepper
4 skinless, boneless chicken breast halves or thighs, 7oz (200g) each
peanut or vegetable oil
5½oz (150g) thin, rice-stick noodles

For the dipping sauce

4 garlic cloves, finely grated
4 fresh hot red chili peppers, seeded and finely chopped
1 tbsp rice wine vinegar
pinch of granulated sugar
juice of 1 lemon

METHOD

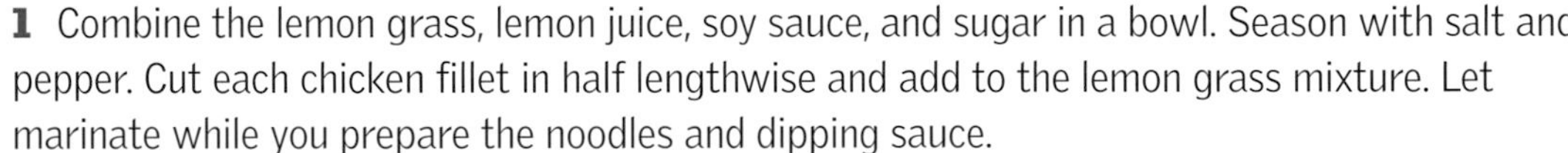

1 Combine the lemon grass, lemon juice, soy sauce, and sugar in a bowl. Season with salt and pepper. Cut each chicken fillet in half lengthwise and add to the lemon grass mixture. Let marinate while you prepare the noodles and dipping sauce.

2 Prepare the rice noodles as the package directs; drain and keep warm.

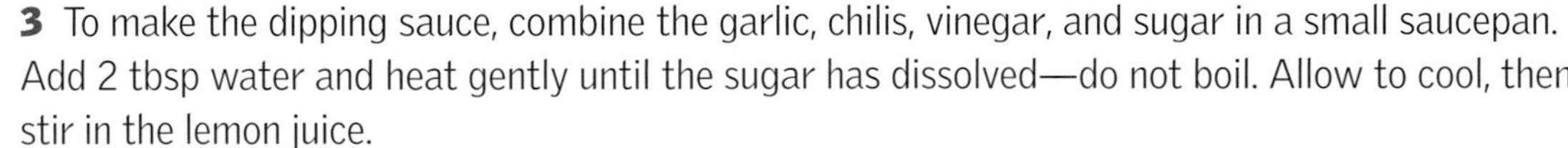

3 To make the dipping sauce, combine the garlic, chilis, vinegar, and sugar in a small saucepan. Add 2 tbsp water and heat gently until the sugar has dissolved—do not boil. Allow to cool, then stir in the lemon juice.

4 Thread the chicken lengthwise onto 8 medium skewers, allowing two for each serving. Heat a ridged cast-iron grill pan or frying pan until hot. Brush lightly with oil, and grill the chicken for 3–4 minutes on each side until cooked through and lightly charred. Serve with the dipping sauce and the rice noodles.

PREPARE AHEAD The dipping sauce can be made several hours in advance. Chill until needed, then bring back to room temperature and stir before serving.

4 servings

prep 15 mins • cook 10 mins

healthy option

if using wooden or bamboo skewers, soak them for 30 mins before use

8 skewers

Classic Chinese wontons

Wontons are healthy and great to have ready in the freezer.

INGREDIENTS

6oz (175g) ground pork
2 scallions, white and green parts, finely chopped
4oz (115g) shiitake mushrooms, stemmed and finely chopped
½in (1cm) piece fresh ginger, peeled and shredded
½ tsp Asian sesame oil
1 tbsp chopped cilantro
1 tbsp soy sauce
freshly ground pepper
1 large egg, beaten
20 wonton wrappers
cornstarch, for the baking sheet
lettuce or napa cabbage

METHOD

1 Mix the pork, scallions, mushrooms, ginger, sesame oil, cilantro, soy sauce, and pepper.

2 Spoon 1 tsp of the pork mixture into the center of a wrapper. Brush the edges lightly with egg, fold the wrapper in half, and crimp the edges to seal. Transfer to a cornstarch-dusted baking sheet.

3 Fill a large saucepan about one-fourth full of water and bring to a boil. Line a steamer with lettuce and add the wontons. Place the steamer on a rack so it sits above the water. Cover and steam the dumplings for 10 minutes, or until cooked through. Serve at once.

GOOD WITH Soy sauce or your favorite dipping sauce.

PREPARE AHEAD The wontons can be covered with plastic wrap and refrigerated several hours in advance.

makes 20

prep 20 mins • cook 10 mins

steamer, bamboo preferred, and a wire rack

freeze, uncooked, for up to 1 month

Baked white fish in wine and herbs

You can use any white fish for this dish, such as haddock, pollack, turbot, or sustainable cod.

INGREDIENTS

1½lb (675g) white fish, skinned and cut into 4 pieces
salt
¾ cup dry white wine
12 cherry tomatoes
handful of parsley, finely chopped

METHOD

1 Preheat the oven to 375°F (190°C). Season the fish with salt, then lay in a single layer in an oven-proof dish. Pour in the wine, and top with the tomatoes and herbs.

2 Cover the dish tightly with foil, then bake for 15–20 minutes until the fish is cooked through and the wine has evaporated.

GOOD WITH A salad and fresh crusty bread for a summery dish, or creamy mashed potatoes for winter.

Couscous with pine nuts and almonds

A tasty alternative to rice; serve either hot or cold.

INGREDIENTS

1 cup couscous
1 red bell pepper, seeded and chopped
1/2 cup raisins
1/2 cup chopped dried apricots
1/2 cucumber, seeded and diced
1/4 cup chopped pitted Kalamata olives
1/4 cup blanched almonds, lightly toasted
1/4 cup pine nuts, lightly toasted
1/4 cup olive oil
2 tbsp fresh lemon juice
1 tbsp chopped mint

METHOD

1 Put the couscous in a heat-proof bowl. Add enough boiling water to cover the couscous by 1in (2.5cm). Let stand for 15 minutes, or until the couscous has absorbed all the water. Fluff up the grains with a fork.

2 Stir in the pepper, raisins, apricots, cucumber, olives, almonds, and pine nuts.

3 Whisk together the oil, lemon juice, and mint. Pour over the couscous and toss. Season with salt and pepper. Serve warm, or let cool and serve at room temperature.

GOOD WITH Grilled meats, chicken, or fish.

PREPARE AHEAD The couscous can be prepared several hours ahead and served at room temperature.

4 servings

prep 15 mins, plus standing

Vegetable kebabs

These can be cooked under the broiler or on a barbecue.

INGREDIENTS

1 medium zucchini
1 red bell pepper, seeded
1 green bell pepper, seeded
1 red onion
8 cherry tomatoes
8 button mushrooms
1/3 cup olive oil
1 garlic clove, minced
1/2 tsp dried oregano
pinch of crushed hot red pepper

METHOD

1 Trim the zucchini and cut into 8 chunks. Cut the peppers into 1in (2.5cm) pieces. Peel the onion, and cut into wedges, leaving the root end intact so that the wedges do not fall apart.

2 Thread the zucchini, peppers, onion, tomatoes, and mushrooms in equal amounts onto 4 large or 8 small skewers. Whisk the oil, garlic, oregano, and hot pepper together in a small bowl with a fork.

3 Position a broiler rack 6in (15cm) from the source of heat and preheat the broiler. Place the kebabs on the broiler pan and brush generously with the garlic oil. Broil, turning often and brushing with the remaining oil, for 10–15 minutes, until the vegetables are just tender. Serve hot or at room temperature, with any remaining oil drizzled over the kebabs.

GOOD WITH A leafy salad for a light vegetarian lunch, or alongside grilled meat or fish.

PREPARE AHEAD Steps 1 and 2 can be completed several hours in advance.

4 servings

prep 15 mins
• cook 15 mins

if using wooden or bamboo skewers, soak them for 30 mins before use

4–8 skewers

Egg noodles with lemon grass and herbs

Fresh Asian noodles absorb the flavors they are cooked in.

INGREDIENTS

12oz (350g) fresh Asian-style egg noodles
2 tbsp plus 2 tsp vegetable oil
2 tbsp soy sauce
2 tbsp fresh lemon juice
pinch of sugar
4 scallions, thinly sliced
1 stalk lemon grass
1in (2.5cm) piece of fresh ginger, peeled and shredded
2 tbsp finely chopped chives
2 tbsp chopped cilantro

METHOD

1 Bring a large pot of salted water to a boil over high heat. Add the noodles and cook according to the package directions. Drain, rinse under cold water, and drain again. Toss with 2 tsp of the oil.

2 Mix the soy sauce, lemon juice, and sugar together; set aside. Remove the outer layer of the lemon grass, and cut off the tough top where it meets the tender bottom bulbous end. Cut the tender bulb into very thin slices, then mince finely.

3 Heat the remaining 2 tbsp oil in a wok over high heat. Add the scallions, lemon grass, and ginger and stir-fry for 1 minute, or until very fragrant. Add the noodles and cook, tossing often, for 2 minutes. Stir in the soy sauce mixture and continue cooking for around 2 minutes, or until hot. Add the chives and cilantro and toss well. Serve immediately.

Pea and mint soup

This soup preserves the fresh taste of its ingredients.

INGREDIENTS
2 cups frozen peas
2 cups hot vegetable stock
handful of mint leaves, coarsely chopped
leaves from a few sprigs of thyme
1–2 tbsp crème fraîche (optional)
pinch of freshly grated nutmeg
salt and freshly ground black pepper

METHOD

1 Cover the peas with hot water and let stand for 5 minutes. Drain.

2 Working in batches if needed, process the peas, stock, mint, and thyme in a blender until smooth. Add more stock if the soup is too thick. Season well with salt and pepper, and process again.

3 To serve, stir in the crème fraîche, and top with a pinch of nutmeg. Serve hot or cold.

GOOD WITH Fresh crusty bread.

Spiced orzo with spinach

Orzo is a tiny soup pasta that looks similar to rice. Enjoy it on its own or with Mediterranean-style dishes.

INGREDIENTS

8oz (225g) orzo
1½ tbsp olive oil
1 onion, finely chopped
2 garlic cloves, finely chopped
1 tsp ground coriander
½ tsp ground cumin
pinch of cayenne (optional)
6oz (175g) baby spinach leaves, washed, but not dried
4 tbsp chopped cilantro or parsley
salt and freshly ground black pepper

METHOD

1 Bring a large pan of salted water to a boil. Add the orzo and cook until tender, according to the package instructions.

2 Meanwhile, heat the olive oil in a large saucepan over medium heat. Add the onion and cook, stirring often, about 3 minutes, until softened. Stir in the garlic, coriander, cumin, and cayenne, if using, and cook for 1 minute more.

3 Stir the spinach (with the water clinging to its leaves from washing) into the saucepan. Cook, stirring often, for 3 minutes, or just until wilted.

4 Drain the orzo well, shaking off any excess water. Add the orzo to the spinach mixture and mix well. Stir in the cilantro and season with salt and pepper. Transfer to a serving bowl. Serve hot or cooled.

PREPARE AHEAD The dish can be refrigerated for up to 1 day, and served cold. If the mixture is too solid, toss with more olive oil.

Kasha pilaf

This is a fragrant and tasty Middle-Eastern-style dish.

INGREDIENTS

2 tbsp butter
1 large onion, chopped
2 celery stalks, sliced
1⅓ cups kasha (buckwheat groats)
1 large egg
1 tsp ground sage
1 tsp ground thyme
¾ cup raisins
¾ cup coarsely chopped walnuts
salt

METHOD

1 Melt the butter in a large frying pan over medium heat. Add the onion and celery and cook for about 3 minutes, or until the vegetables begin to soften.

2 Mix the kasha and egg in a bowl. Add to the frying pan and cook, stirring constantly, about 1 minute, or until the grains are dry and separated. Add 2 cups of water, the sage, and thyme. Increase the heat to high and bring to a boil. Cover and reduce the heat to medium-low. Simmer for about 12 minutes, or until it is almost tender.

3 Stir in the raisins and walnuts. Continue cooking for about 5 minutes, or until the kasha is tender and all the liquid has been absorbed. Season with salt.

4–6 servings

prep 5 mins • cook 25 mins

FROM THE PANTRY

Lentil, fava bean, and feta salad

A healthy, substantial salad that is sure to satisfy any hunger pangs.

INGREDIENTS

$\frac{1}{2}$ cup frozen shelled fava beans
one 14oz (400g) can of green or brown lentils, drained and rinsed, or 2 cups drained cooked lentils
1 bunch of scallions, finely chopped
1 fresh green chili, finely chopped
6oz (175g) feta cheese, cut into cubes
handful of parsley, finely chopped
salt and freshly ground black pepper

For the dressing

3 tbsp olive oil
1 tbsp white wine vinegar
one 1in (2.5cm) piece fresh ginger, peeled and grated
pinch of sugar (optional)

METHOD

1 Cover the fava beans with boiling water and let sit for 5 minutes. Drain.

2 Put the lentils in a serving bowl and season with a pinch of salt and some pepper. Stir in the drained fava beans, scallions, and chili.

3 To make the dressing, combine the oil, vinegar, and ginger in a small bowl. Season with salt and pepper and a pinch of sugar (if using), and whisk until well blended. Drizzle over the salad and let stand for 10 minutes, to allow the flavors to develop.

4 When ready to serve, stir in the feta and parsley.

Vegetarian Pad Thai

This popular Thai noodle dish is made more substantial by adding tofu.

INGREDIENTS

9oz (250g) wide or medium rice noodles
3–4 tbsp vegetable oil
8oz (225g) firm tofu, diced
2 garlic cloves, finely chopped
1 large egg, lightly beaten
2/3 cup hot vegetable stock
juice of 1 lime
1 tsp Asian fish sauce, such as nam pla (optional)
2 tsp tamarind paste
2 tsp demerara or raw sugar
1 tbsp soy sauce
1 fresh hot red chili pepper, seeded and finely chopped
1/3 cup dry-roasted peanuts, coarsely chopped
1 bunch of scallions, finely chopped
1 cup fresh bean sprouts (optional)
handful of cilantro leaves

METHOD

1 Soak the rice noodles in a bowl of boiling hot water for 10 minutes, then drain. Heat 1 tbsp of the vegetable oil in a wok over medium-high heat, and swirl it around the pan. Add the tofu, and cook for about 10 minutes until golden—you may need to use more oil. Remove with a slotted spoon and set aside.

2 Add another 1 tbsp of oil to the pan. When hot, add the garlic and cook for 10 seconds, then add the egg and cook, stirring and breaking it up with a wooden spoon, until scrambled. Remove from the pan, and set aside.

3 Now add another 1 tbsp of oil. Again, when hot, add the drained noodles, and stir gently to coat with the oil. Pour in the stock, lime juice, fish sauce (if using), tamarind paste, sugar, and soy sauce; toss to combine. Let bubble for a few minutes, then stir in the chili.

4 Add half of the peanuts, the scallions, and the bean sprouts, and stir-fry for 1 minute. Now top with the reserved scrambled egg, stir to combine, and transfer to a serving plate. To serve, scatter the remaining peanuts over the top, and sprinkle with cilantro.

Linguine with tomato clam sauce

Versions of this popular classic shellfish dish of thin linguine and clams are cooked all along the Italian Mediterranean and Adriatic coasts.

INGREDIENTS

2 tbsp olive oil
1 onion, finely chopped
2 garlic cloves, finely chopped
one 28oz (794g) can chopped tomatoes
two 6½oz (184g) cans clams in natural juice, drained, juice reserved
¾ cup dry white wine
2 tbsp tomato paste
salt and freshly ground black pepper
1lb (450g) dried linguine
4 tbsp finely chopped parsley, plus more to garnish

METHOD

1 Heat the oil in a large saucepan over medium heat. Add the onion and cook, stirring frequently, for 5 minutes, or until softened. Add the garlic and stir until fragrant, about 1 minute. Add the tomatoes with their juices, clam juices, wine, and tomato paste. Season with salt and pepper. Bring to a boil. Reduce the heat to low, partially cover the pan and simmer for 10–15 minutes, until the sauce thickens, stirring occasionally.

2 Meanwhile, bring a large pot of salted water to a boil over high heat. Stir in the linguine, and cook according to the package directions, or until *al dente*. Drain the pasta, and shake to remove any excess water.

3 When the pasta is almost done, add the clams and chopped parsley to the tomato sauce and continue to simmer for 1–2 minutes, until heated through. Add salt and pepper to taste.

4 Add the linguine to the sauce, and toss to combine all the ingredients, so the clams are well distributed throughout the pasta. Sprinkle with extra parsley and serve at once.

GOOD WITH Crusty Italian bread.

[illegible]uccine Alfredo

[illegible]unsurpassable dish made with good-quality ingredients.

[illegible]GREDIENTS

[illegible]o (450g) dried fettucine
3 tbsp butter, cubed
1 cup heavy cream
½ cup freshly grated Parmesan, plus more for serving
salt and freshly ground black pepper

THE PANTRY

METHOD

1 Bring a large saucepan of lightly salted water to a boil over high heat. Add the fettuccine and cook according to the package instructions, just until *al dente*.

2 Meanwhile, melt the butter in a large saucepan over low heat. Add the cream and heat until steaming. Drain the fettuccine well, and add to the hot cream mixture. Add the Parmesan and toss well to coat. Season with salt and pepper.

3 Divide the pasta among warmed plates. Serve at once, with more grated Parmesan passed on the side, or shave curls from a chunk of Parmesan over each serving.

4 servings

prep 5 mins
• cook 15 mins

Rice balls filled with cheese

A great way of using up leftover rice, these little snacks are very satisfying.

INGREDIENTS

salt
1¼ cup cold, cooked Arborio or other risotto rice
2 balls of fresh mozzarella cheese, cubed
1 egg, beaten
½ cup fresh bread crumbs, toasted
olive oil, for frying

METHOD

1 Generously season the cold risotto rice with salt, then roll it into 12 even-sized balls.

2 Push a cube of mozzarella into the center of each ball, then cover so that the cheese is enclosed.

3 Roll each ball first in the beaten egg, then in the toasted bread crumbs. Heat some olive oil in a frying pan over medium heat and fry each ball for 2–5 minutes, or until golden. Serve hot.

4 servings

prep 25 mins • cook 5 mins

Spaetzle

When tossed with cheese and eggs, spaetzle, a homemade noodle from Switzerland, makes a delicious one-pot meal.

INGREDIENTS

3 cups all-purpose flour
6 large eggs
½ cup whole milk, as needed
½ tsp freshly grated nutmeg
4 tbsp butter
1 cup shredded Gruyère cheese
freshly ground black pepper
2 scallions, white and green parts, finely chopped

METHOD

1 Sift the flour into a bowl. Lightly beat 4 eggs with ½ cup water, the milk, and nutmeg. Add to the flour, mixing to make a thick batter, adding more milk if necessary.

2 Bring a large saucepan of water to a boil over high heat. Transfer the batter to a colander with large holes. Rub the batter through the holes with a rubber spatula, letting the batter drop into the hot water (be sure to protect your hands from the steam).

3 Cook for 2–3 minutes, or until all of the spaetzle are floating. Drain and rinse under cold running water.

4 Heat the butter in a large frying pan over medium-high heat. Add the spaetzle and cook, stirring occasionally, 3 minutes, until they are beginning to brown. Reduce the heat to low. Beat the remaining 2 eggs. Sprinkle in the cheese and eggs and stir for 1–2 minutes until the cheese melts and the eggs are set. Season with pepper. Sprinkle with the scallions and serve hot.

4 servings

prep 20 mins • cook 10 mins

colander with large holes

Tomato bulgur wheat with capers and olives

This dish gives Middle-Eastern bulgur wheat a Mediterranean character.

INGREDIENTS

2 cups bulgur wheat
salt and freshly ground black pepper
$^2/_3$–$1^1/_4$ cups tomato juice
1 tbsp capers, drained
12 black olives, such as Kalamata, pitted and halved
12 green olives, pitted and halved

METHOD

1 Pour the bulgur wheat into a large heat-proof bowl, then pour in just enough boiling water to cover—about $1^1/_4$ cups. Let stand for 15 minutes.

2 Season generously with salt and pepper, and stir well with a fork to fluff up the grains. Add the tomato juice, a little at a time, until the bulgur has absorbed all the juice. Let stand for a few minutes between each addition—the bulgur will absorb quite a lot of moisture.

3 Now add the capers and olives, taste, and season again if needed.

GOOD WITH A crisp green salad and some warm pita bread.

Pasta with sun-dried tomato pesto

Homemade pesto has a wonderful, fresh taste and is very quick to make.

INGREDIENTS

½ of a 10oz (300g) jar sun-dried tomatoes in oil, drained
handful of pine nuts
2 garlic cloves, coarsely chopped
handful of fresh basil leaves, plus extra for garnish
½ cup freshly grated Parmesan cheese, or as needed
extra-virgin olive oil
12oz (350g) dried fusilli
salt and freshly ground black pepper

METHOD

1 Combine the sun-dried tomatoes, pine nuts, garlic, basil, and ½ cup Parmesan in a food processor. Pulse until blended. Season with salt and pepper. Taste and add more Parmesan and a splash of oil, as needed.

2 Meanwhile, cook the pasta as the package directs, or until *al dente*. Drain, reserving a small amount of the cooking water. Return the pasta to the pot and toss together with the reserved cooking water. Add the pesto and toss again. Drizzle with extra-virgin olive oil, garnish with basil leaves, and serve.

PREPARE AHEAD The pesto can be made several days in advance. Spoon it into a jar and top with a thin layer of olive oil—it will keep in the refrigerator for up to 1 week.

Tuna and white beans with olives

A speedy no-cook dish with clean, Mediterranean flavors.

INGREDIENTS

one 14oz (400g) can butter beans, drained
one 14oz (400g) can cannellini beans, drained
two 7oz (200g) cans tuna in olive oil, drained
2 tbsp white wine vinegar
salt and freshly ground black pepper
1 tsp whole-grain mustard
½ tsp mild paprika
about 12 black olives, such as Kalamata, pitted and halved
2 tsp capers, drained

METHOD

1 Combine all the beans and the tuna in a large bowl. Add the vinegar, taste, and season well with salt and pepper.

2 Stir in the mustard, paprika, olives, and capers. Taste, and season again if needed. Serve immediately.

PREPARE AHEAD The completed dish can be refrigerated for a couple of hours until needed. Bring back to room temperature before serving.

Pasta with Pecorino and peas

Pecorino's bold, salty flavor adds character to a simple sauce; if you don't have it, Parmesan works well—just use a little less.

INGREDIENTS

1 tbsp olive oil
1 onion, finely chopped
1 garlic clove, finely chopped
1 fresh red jalapeño chili pepper, seeded and finely chopped
2 tsp all-purpose flour
1/4 cup dry white wine
2/3 cup whole milk
1 cup frozen peas
1 cup freshly grated Pecorino cheese, plus extra for serving
12oz (350g) dried farfalle pasta
salt and freshly ground black pepper

METHOD

1 Heat the oil in a large frying pan, add the onion and a pinch of salt, and cook over low heat for 5 minutes, or until soft. Stir in the garlic and chili and cook for a few seconds more. Stir in the flour until well blended, then add the wine, and allow to bubble for a couple of minutes. Stir in the milk.

2 Stir in the peas, then add the Pecorino and cook at a low simmer—do not allow to boil—for 10 minutes or until the sauce has thickened slightly. Season well with salt and pepper.

3 Meanwhile, cook the pasta according to package directions, or until *al dente*. Drain, reserving a small amount of the cooking water. Return the pasta to the pot and toss together with the reserved cooking water. Add the sauce, toss again, top with extra Pecorino, and serve.

Lentils with artichokes and peppers

Juicy, crunchy, salty, and sweet—this quick, filling salad has it all.

INGREDIENTS

one 14oz (400g) can green or brown lentils, drained and rinsed, or 2 cups drained cooked lentils
one 14oz (400g) can artichoke hearts, drained and sliced
4 or 5 roasted red peppers from a jar or the deli counter
leaves from 1–2 thyme sprigs
handful of parsley, chopped
4 scallions, finely chopped
2–3 tbsp walnut oil
1 tbsp cider vinegar
4 or 5 thin slices Parma ham or other prosciutto, chopped
handful of wild arugula leaves

METHOD

1 Put the lentils, artichoke hearts, peppers, thyme, parsley, and scallions in a bowl. Drizzle the oil and vinegar over the top, and toss gently to mix.

2 Toss in the ham and arugula. Transfer to a serving dish and serve with a green salad.

Gnocchi with Gorgonzola and walnut sauce

Blue cheese and walnuts are a classic pairing and make this Italian dish something special.

INGREDIENTS

1 tbsp butter
1 onion, finely chopped
1/3 cup coarsely chopped walnuts
1 tbsp all-purpose flour
2 cups whole milk
4 1/2oz (125g) Gorgonzola cheese
1 package (about 18oz/500g) fresh or frozen gnocchi
salt and freshly ground black pepper
handful of basil leaves, to garnish (optional)

METHOD

1 In a saucepan, melt the butter over low heat. Add the onion, and cook gently for about 5 minutes until soft. Now add the walnuts, and cook for another couple of minutes. Remove from the heat, and stir in the flour, then add a little milk. Return to the heat, and add the remaining milk, stirring constantly for 4–6 minutes until the sauce thickens.

2 Remove from the heat again, and stir in the Gorgonzola. Season with salt and pepper.

3 In a separate saucepan, cook the gnocchi as the package directs. Drain well. Add to the sauce, stirring gently to coat. Garnish with the basil leaves (if using), and serve immediately.

GOOD WITH A tomato and arugula salad.

Egg fu yung

Light and tasty, these are made with shrimp and stir-fried vegetables.

INGREDIENTS

vegetable oil, as needed
3 shallots, thinly sliced
1 green bell pepper, seeded and diced
1 celery stalk, chopped
2 garlic cloves, minced
1 cup bean sprouts
4oz (115g) frozen shrimp, thawed
5 eggs, beaten
¾ cup vegetable stock
1 tbsp oyster sauce
1 tbsp soy sauce
1 tbsp Chinese rice wine or sherry
2 tsp cornstarch
boiled rice, to serve

METHOD

1 Heat 2 tbsp oil in a wok over high heat. Add the shallots, bell pepper, celery, and garlic and stir-fry for 3 minutes. Add the bean sprouts, stir-fry for 1 minute, then add the shrimp and stir-fry for 1 minute, or until the shrimp turn pink. Transfer to a bowl and let cool.

2 Add the beaten eggs, stirring until well combined. Wash the wok and wipe it dry with paper towels.

3 Return the wok to high heat and pour in 2in (5cm) oil. When the oil is hot, ladle ¼ of the mixture into the oil. Fry about 2 minutes, until the underside is lightly browned, spooning a little of the hot oil over the eggs so the top starts to set.

4 Carefully turn the egg cake over and cook 1 minute, until lightly browned on the other side. Transfer to paper towels to drain. Keep warm in a 200°F (95°C) oven while making the remaining cakes.

5 Meanwhile, mix the stock, oyster sauce, soy sauce, and rice wine in a saucepan. Dissolve the cornstarch in 2 tbsp cold water, and stir into the stock mixture. Bring to a boil over high heat, stirring constantly until thickened; simmer for 1 minute. Serve the cakes with the sauce and rice.

4 servings

prep 15 mins
• cook 20 mins

wok

Bean burgers

A tasty and low-fat alternative to burgers made with meat.

INGREDIENTS

one 15oz (425g) can aduki beans, drained and rinsed
one 15½oz (440g) can chickpeas, drained and rinsed
1 onion, coarsely chopped
6 anchovies in olive oil, drained
1 tbsp coarse-grained mustard
salt and freshly ground black pepper
2 large eggs, lightly beaten
2–3 tbsp all-purpose flour, plus extra for dusting
2–3 tbsp vegetable or sunflower oil

METHOD

1 Put the drained beans in a food processor, and pulse the machine on and off several times until coarsely chopped. Add the onion, anchovies, and mustard, and season well with salt and pepper. Pulse a few times more. You want the mixture to be well combined, but not puréed. Now add the eggs, and pulse again until blended. Add 2–3 tbsp flour to bind the burgers, and pulse until incorporated.

2 Heat 1 tbsp of the oil in a large nonstick frying pan over medium heat. Once the oil is hot, spoon out a portion of the bean mixture (there is enough to make 6 burgers) and, using well-floured hands, form into a patty just before adding to the pan. Working in batches, cook 2 or 3 patties at a time for 4–6 minutes, turning only once, until firm and golden. Add more oil to the pan as needed. Set aside and keep the burgers warm as you cook the remaining patties. Serve hot.

GOOD WITH A toasted hamburger bun, crisp lettuce, and ketchup.

4–6 servings

prep 15 mins • cook 10 mins

healthy option

food processor

freeze, uncooked, for up to 1 month

Paneer and peas

This Indian restaurant favorite is easy to make at home. If you can't find paneer, farmer's cheese is a good substitute.

INGREDIENTS

6 tbsp vegetable oil
1 large onion, thinly sliced
2 large garlic cloves, coarsely chopped
1 fresh hot green chili, seeds and ribs removed and chopped
one ½in (1cm) piece fresh ginger, peeled and coarsely chopped
2 tsp garam masala
salt and freshly ground black pepper
one 14½oz (411g) can crushed tomatoes
one 1lb (450g) bag frozen peas
8oz (225g) paneer, cut into bite-sized cubes

METHOD

1 Heat 3 tbsp of the oil in a large nonstick frying pan over medium-high heat. Add the onion and reduce the heat to medium-low. Cook, stirring frequently for 8–10 minutes or until the onions are dark golden brown; do not burn.

2 Meanwhile, combine the garlic, chili, and ginger in a blender and process into a thick paste. Add the garam masala and season with salt and pepper.

3 Add the spice mixture to the fried onions and cook, stirring, for 1–2 minutes. Transfer to a large, heavy-bottomed saucepan. Stir in the tomatoes and ⅔ cup water. Bring to a boil, stirring often. Reduce the heat to low and simmer, stirring often, until lightly thickened.

4 Gently stir the frozen peas into the sauce, increase the heat to medium, and return the sauce to a simmer. Cover and cook for about 5 minutes, or until the peas are hot.

5 Wash and dry the frying pan. Add 3 tbsp oil and heat over high heat. In batches, add the paneer in a single layer. Cook, turning occasionally with a slotted spatula, about 3 minutes or until golden brown. Transfer the fried paneer to the hot tomato sauce. Continue with the remaining paneer, adding more oil as needed.

GOOD WITH Hot chapatis.

Pasta with olives, capers, and sun-dried tomatoes

Preserved ingredients have deeper, more intense flavors, as well as being convenient.

INGREDIENTS

12oz (350g) dried penne or pasta of your choice
1 tbsp olive oil
3 tsp capers, rinsed and gently squeezed dry
handful of black olives, pitted
6 sun-dried tomatoes in oil, drained and chopped (reserve a little of the oil, optional)
salt and freshly ground black pepper

METHOD

1 Cook the pasta according to the package directions, or until *al dente*. Drain, reserving a small amount of the cooking water. Return the pasta to the pot and toss together with the reserved cooking water.

2 Meanwhile, in another pan, heat the olive oil over low heat. Add the capers, olives, and sun-dried tomatoes, and cook gently for about 5 minutes, mashing them slightly with the back of a fork.

3 Scrape the mixture into the cooked pasta, and toss until evenly mixed. Add a little of the reserved oil from the sun-dried tomatoes. Season well with salt and pepper, and serve at once.

4 servings

prep 10 mins
• cook 15 mins

Welsh rarebit

Often pronounced as Welsh "rabbit," this simple recipe makes a meal out of Cheddar or Lancashire cheese.

INGREDIENTS

4 slices white or whole-wheat bread
2 tbsp butter
2 cups (8oz/225g) shredded sharp Cheddar
  or Lancashire cheese
3 tbsp dark ale, porter, or lager
1 tbsp dry mustard
Worcestershire sauce

METHOD

1 Line a baking sheet with aluminum foil. Position the broiler rack 4in (10cm) from the heat, and preheat. Toast the bread on both sides until golden brown. Transfer the toast to the baking sheet.

2 Melt the butter in a saucepan over low heat. Add the cheese, ale, and mustard and cook, stirring often, until the cheese is melted and smooth.

3 Pour the sauce over the toast. Splash a few drops of Worcestershire sauce on each. Return the cheese-covered toast to the broiler for a few minutes, or until the cheese is bubbling and golden. Cut each slice in half and serve.

GOOD WITH Salad. If desired, put cooked ham under the cheese sauce before grilling.

4 servings

prep 10 mins • cook 6 mins

the cheese sauce is runny, so line the baking sheet with aluminum foil before baking

Rice and black-eyed peas

Coconut and chilis give this Caribbean-inspired dish a rich, spicy flavor.

INGREDIENTS

1 tbsp olive oil
1 onion, finely chopped
2 garlic cloves, finely chopped
2–3 fresh hot chili peppers, seeded and finely chopped
2½ cups long-grain white rice, rinsed
one 14oz (400g) can black-eyed peas, drained and rinsed
one 14oz (400g) can unsweetened coconut milk
3 cups hot vegetable stock, or as needed

METHOD

1 Heat the oil in a saucepan over low heat and cook the onion for 5 minutes until soft. Add the garlic and chilis, and cook for a few seconds more.

2 Stir in the rice, making sure the grains are well coated, then add the beans, coconut milk, and most of the stock. Cover the pan, and cook over low heat for about 20 minutes until all the liquid has been absorbed and the rice is tender; if you need to add more stock, do so. Serve hot.

GOOD WITH Freshly steamed, boiled, or sautéed vegetables.

HEARTY AND FILLING

Lamb koftas

Middle Eastern spices flavor these tender, ground lamb kebabs. A raita of cucumber and yogurt is the ideal accompaniment

INGREDIENTS

1 slice of white bread, crusts discarded, torn into small pieces
3 tbsp whole milk
1lb (450g) ground lamb
1 tbsp chopped cilantro
1 tbsp chopped parsley
1 tbsp ground cumin
1 garlic clove, minced to a purée
1/2 tsp salt
1/2 tsp freshly ground black pepper
vegetable oil, for brushing

For the raita

1 1/2 cups plain yogurt
4oz (115g) cucumber, peeled, seeded, and diced

METHOD

1 Soak the bread in the milk for 5 minutes.

2 Combine the ground lamb, cilantro, parsley, cumin, garlic, salt, and pepper in a large bowl. Squeeze the milk from the bread, add the bread to the bowl and mix thoroughly with your hands. Discard any remaining milk.

3 Using wet hands, roll the mixture into 16 balls. Carefully slide each ball onto a skewer.

4 Meanwhile, preheat the broiler and position the rack about 4in (10cm) from the source of heat. Line the broiler pan with aluminum foil and lightly oil.

5 Put the koftas on the pan and broil, turning frequently, for about 8 minutes for medium-rare, or 10 minutes for well done. Transfer to a platter. Mix the yogurt and cucumber with a little salt to taste and serve on the side.

PREPARE AHEAD The shaped koftas can be refrigerated up to 1 day before cooking. The sauce can be made an hour or two in advance.

makes 16

prep 15 mins, plus chilling • cook 8–10 mins

if using wooden or bamboo skewers, soak them for 30 mins before use

16 skewers

Chicken fajitas with tomato and avocado salsa

This speedy version of the Mexican favorite uses clever shortcuts to achieve the flavors of the original.

INGREDIENTS

1 tbsp olive oil
2 onions, halved and sliced
2 red bell peppers, seeded and cut into strips
2 green bell peppers, seeded and cut into strips
2 fresh red jalapeño chili peppers, seeded and finely chopped
2 garlic cloves, thinly sliced
4 skinless, boneless chicken breast halves (preferably free-range), about 6oz (175g) each, cut into strips
1/2 cup dry white wine
8–12 corn tortillas, warmed
handful of cilantro, finely chopped

For the salsa

1 ripe avocado
handful of cherry tomatoes, chopped
1 bunch of scallions, finely chopped
handful of parsley, finely chopped
1 tbsp olive oil
1 tbsp white wine vinegar
salt and freshly ground black pepper

METHOD

1 First, make the salsa. Halve, pit, peel, and chop the avocado. Put in a bowl with the tomatoes, scallions, and parsley. Drizzle in the olive oil and vinegar. Season with salt and pepper and stir to mix.

2 To make the chicken fajitas, heat the oil in a large hot frying pan over low heat. Add the onions and red and green bell peppers, and sauté for 5 minutes until soft. Stir in the chilis and garlic, and cook briefly.

3 Increase the heat to medium-high and add the chicken. Keep the mixture moving around the pan, so that it doesn't burn and the chicken is evenly cooked. Stir-fry for 3–5 minutes until the chicken is no longer pink. Pour in the wine, and cook for 5 minutes. Stir in the cilantro.

4 To serve, spoon the mixture onto the tortillas. Top with the salsa, and roll into wraps. Serve any extra filling on the side.

GOOD WITH Sour cream as an extra sauce.

4 servings

prep 15 mins • cook 15 mins

Danish meatballs

Any meat variety works well in this recipe.

INGREDIENTS

1 cup loosely packed fresh bread crumbs
1/3 cup whole milk
1 large egg, beaten
1/2 tsp dried thyme
1 tsp salt
1/4 tsp freshly ground black pepper
9oz (250g) ground pork
9oz (250g) ground turkey or chicken
1 onion, grated
all-purpose flour, for shaping
2 tbsp vegetable oil
lemon wedges, to serve

METHOD

1 Mix the bread crumbs and milk in a medium bowl and let stand for 5 minutes. Mix in the egg, thyme, salt, and pepper.

2 Add the pork, turkey (or chicken), and onion and mix with your hands until well combined. With lightly floured hands, shape into about 16 balls.

3 Heat the oil in a large frying pan over medium heat. Add the meatballs and cook, turning often, for 8–10 minutes, until golden brown.

4 servings

prep 15 mins • cook 10 mins

raw or cooked meatballs can be frozen for up to 3 months

Pork chops with green peppercorn sauce

These soft, mild peppercorns add a gentle spice to the creamy sauce.

INGREDIENTS

4 center-cut pork loin chops
salt and freshly ground black pepper
1 tbsp vegetable oil
2 tbsp butter
1 large shallot, finely chopped
1/4 cup dry sherry
2/3 cup chicken stock
1 1/2 tbsp green peppercorns in brine, rinsed, drained, and lightly crushed
1/4 cup crème fraîche or heavy cream

METHOD

1 Trim the chops of excess fat and season with salt and pepper. Heat the oil in a large, heavy frying pan on medium heat. Add the pork chops and cook for 6–8 minutes on each side, depending on thickness, until golden brown and the juices run clear. Transfer to a warm plate and cover with foil.

2 To make the sauce, melt the butter in the pan. Add the shallot and cook, stirring often, for about 2 minutes, or until tender. Add the sherry, and cook for 1 minute, stirring up the browned pieces in the pan. Add the stock and peppercorns and cook about 2 minutes, or until slightly reduced.

3 Stir in the crème fraîche. Spoon the sauce over the chops and serve immediately.

GOOD WITH Potato rösti cakes and steamed green vegetables.

PREPARE AHEAD The sauce can be made up to 2 days in advance, cooled, covered, and refrigerated.

4 servings

prep 10 mins • cook 15 mins

Kidneys with mustard sauce

This makes a hearty and wholesome supper dish.

INGREDIENTS

4 lamb kidneys
2 tbsp butter
1 tbsp olive oil
1 large onion, finely chopped
2 garlic cloves, minced
8 cremini mushrooms, sliced
3 tbsp dry vermouth or red wine
4 tbsp lamb or beef stock
2 tsp Dijon mustard
salt and freshly ground black pepper

METHOD

1 Peel away any skin from the kidneys and cut out the core and membranes. Soak in water to cover for 5–10 minutes. Drain and pat dry with paper towels.

2 Heat the butter and oil in a frying pan over medium heat. Cook the onion, stirring often, for 2–3 minutes. Increase the heat, add the kidneys and garlic, and cook for 3 minutes, stirring.

3 Add the mushrooms, and cook for 2–3 minutes more. Add the vermouth and stock and boil about 1 minute, until slightly reduced.

4 Reduce the heat and cover. Cook for 4 minutes, or until the kidneys are tender and cooked through. Stir in the mustard and season with salt and pepper.

GOOD WITH Slices of toasted whole-wheat bread.

4 servings

prep 10 mins, plus soaking • cook 11–15 mins

Lamb with blueberries

Tender lamb noisettes (filet mignons) are a special treat.

INGREDIENTS

12 lamb noisettes, cut 1½in (3cm) thick
salt and freshly ground black pepper
2 tbsp olive oil
3 scallions, chopped
⅔ cup lamb or chicken stock
1½ tbsp red currant jelly
1 cup blueberries
2 tbsp finely chopped mint plus sprigs, to garnish

METHOD

1 Season the lamb with salt and pepper. Heat 1 tbsp oil in a large, heavy-bottomed frying pan over high heat. Cook the lamb in batches for 3–4 minutes on each side, until browned and medium-rare. Transfer to a plate and tent with foil to keep warm.

2 Add 1 tbsp of the oil to the pan. Add the scallions and cook for 2–3 minutes. Stir in the stock and jelly and cook until the jelly is dissolved and the liquid boils.

3 Add the blueberries and simmer, uncovered, for 2 minutes, then add the mint.

4 Transfer the lamb to dinner plates and spoon the sauce on top. Serve immediately.

4 servings

prep 10 mins
• cook 8–12 mins

Wasabi beef and bok choy

Similar in taste to horseradish, wasabi is popular in Japanese cooking, and is superb with beef.

INGREDIENTS

2 tbsp olive oil
2 tsp wasabi paste
4 sirloin steaks, about 7oz (200g) each
7oz (200g) bok choy, cut lengthwise into 8 pieces
5 garlic cloves, finely chopped
1 tbsp soy sauce
salt and freshly ground black pepper

METHOD

1 Heat a ridged cast-iron grill pan until it is hot. Mix together 1 tbsp of the olive oil and the wasabi paste. Use the mixture to coat the sirloin steaks thinly and evenly.

2 Put the steaks on the grill pan and grill over high heat for about 3 minutes on each side. Transfer to a plate, and leave to rest in a warm place for 5 minutes.

3 Meanwhile, toss the bok choy in the remaining olive oil with the garlic and soy sauce. Grill on the grill pan for 2–3 minutes until charred and just wilted.

4 To serve, cut the steak into 1/2in (1cm) slices and serve with the bok choy.

4 servings

prep 10 mins • cook 10 mins

ridged cast-iron grill pan

Mussels in fennel broth

This fragrant broth with coconut and juicy mussels makes an impressive dish.

INGREDIENTS

1 tbsp olive oil
1 onion, finely chopped
1 fennel bulb, trimmed and finely chopped
2 garlic cloves, finely chopped
2 all-purpose waxy potatoes, peeled and finely diced
$1\frac{1}{4}$ cups hot vegetable stock or light fish stock
one 14oz (400ml) can unsweetened coconut milk
3lb (1.35kg) fresh mussels, cleaned
handful of fresh basil leaves, torn
salt and freshly ground black pepper

METHOD

1 Heat the oil in a saucepan over low heat. Add the onion, fennel, and salt, then cook for 5 minutes until softened. Stir in the garlic and potatoes, and cook for 2 minutes until well coated.

2 Pour in the stock and bring to a boil. Stir in the coconut milk, reduce the heat slightly, and simmer gently for about 10 minutes. Bring back to a boil, add the mussels, and cover the pan. Cook for about 5 minutes until the mussels are open (discard any that do not open).

3 To serve, stir in the basil, taste the broth, and season if needed. Serve hot.

GOOD WITH Fresh crusty bread to mop up the broth.

4 servings

prep 10 mins • cook 20 mins

before cooking, tap the mussels and discard any that do not close

Boudin noir and sautéed apples

Boudin noir (literally "black sausage") and apples is a classic combination in French cooking. In Latino markets, it is called morcilla or morcela

INGREDIENTS

3 Golden Delicious apples, peeled, cored, and thickly sliced
2 tbsp butter
2 tsp light brown sugar
2 tsp vegetable oil
8 large slices of boudin noir
4 slices bacon, cut lengthwise into thin strips
½ cup hard cider

METHOD

1 Cut each apple slice in half crosswise. Melt the butter in a frying pan over medium heat. Add the apples and brown sugar. Cook, stirring often, for 8–10 minutes, until the apples are softened and slightly caramelized. Transfer to a plate and tent with aluminum foil to keep warm.

2 Wipe out the pan. Add the oil and heat over medium-high heat. In batches, add the boudin noir and cook, turning once, for about 6 minutes, until slightly crisp. Transfer to the plate. Add the bacon to the frying pan and cook, stirring frequently, for about 3 minutes, or until cooked through and slightly crisp. Transfer to the plate. Add the cider to the pan and increase the heat to high. Boil until reduced and syrupy, stirring up the browned pieces in the pan wth a wooden spoon.

3 To serve, place a slice of boudin noir on each of 4 plates. Add a layer of apples, then repeat with the remaining boudin noir and apples. Top with the bacon strips and drizzle with the pan juices.

GOOD WITH Creamy mashed potato.

4 servings

prep 10 mins
• cook 20 mins

Baked flounder with bacon

This is a tasty and unusual way of cooking delicate flounder or sole.

INGREDIENTS

2 tbsp olive oil
4 bacon slices, coarsely chopped
3 scallions, white and green parts, chopped
4 flounder fillets, about 6oz (175g) each
freshly ground pepper
4 tbsp butter
2 tbsp fresh lemon juice
1 tbsp chopped fresh parsley

METHOD

1 Preheat the oven to 400°F (200°C). Heat the oil in a flame-proof roasting pan over medium heat. Add the bacon and scallions, and cook for 2 minutes, stirring frequently. Add the flounder, skin side down, baste with the oil, and season with pepper.

2 Bake for 15 minutes, basting once or twice. Transfer each fillet to a plate. Drain the bacon and scallions in a strainer.

3 Heat the butter in a small saucepan over medium heat about 2 minutes, until golden brown. Add the reserved bacon and scallions with the lemon juice, and stir in the parsley. Spoon over the fish and serve immediately.

GOOD WITH Stir-fried or steamed vegetables, such as spinach, green beans, or carrots.

Minced chicken with exotic mushrooms, soy, and lime

Bring a taste of Asia to your table with this easy dish.

INGREDIENTS

2 or 3 skinless, boneless chicken breast halves, about 7oz (200g) each, coarsely chopped
1 tbsp olive oil
1 onion, finely chopped
1 garlic clove, finely chopped
1 fresh red jalapeño chili pepper, seeded and finely chopped
12oz (350g) mixed fresh exotic or wild mushrooms (such as oyster, shiitake, and enoki), or cultivated mushrooms, finely chopped
3 tbsp soy sauce
juice of 2 limes
handful of cilantro leaves, finely chopped
handful of basil leaves, finely chopped
salt and freshly ground black pepper
hot cooked rice, to serve

METHOD

1 Pulse the chicken in a food processor until finely chopped. Set aside.

2 Heat the oil in a large frying pan over medium heat. Add the onion and a pinch of salt, and cook for 5 minutes until soft. Stir in the garlic and chili, and cook for a few seconds more.

3 Add the chicken to the pan, season well with salt and pepper, and cook, stirring occasionally, for a few minutes until the chicken is no longer pink. Stir in the mushrooms, and cook for about 5 minutes longer.

4 Stir in the soy sauce and lime juice, and cook for 2 minutes. Taste, and season again if needed. Just before serving, stir in the cilantro and basil. Serve immediately with the hot rice, either on the side or mixed together.

4 servings

prep 10 mins • cook 20 mins

food processor

Bulgur with mixed peppers, mint, and paprika

Sweet, crunchy peppers and creamy goat cheese are a winning combination.

INGREDIENTS

1½ cups (250g) fine bulgur (cracked wheat)
about 2 cups low-salt vegetable stock, heated until hot
1 bunch of scallions, finely chopped
1 orange bell pepper, seeded and diced
1 yellow bell pepper, seeded and diced
pinch of paprika
handful of mint leaves, finely chopped
juice of 1 lemon
4–4½oz (125g) soft goat cheese, crumbled (about 1 cup)
drizzle of fruity extra-virgin olive oil
salt and freshly ground black pepper

METHOD

1 Put the bulgur wheat in a large heat-proof bowl, and pour in just enough hot stock to cover. Let stand for 15–20 minutes, until the grains are swollen and the liquid is absorbed. Stir with a fork to fluff up the bulgur. Season well with salt and pepper.

2 Stir in the scallions, peppers, paprika, mint, and lemon juice. Taste, and season again if needed.

3 To serve, top with the goat cheese and a generous drizzle of olive oil.

Asparagus, broccoli, ginger, and mint stir-fry

Take care not to overcook the vegetables—they should remain crunchy and fresh-tasting.

INGREDIENTS

1 tbsp sesame oil or vegetable oil
2 fresh red chili peppers, seeded and finely chopped
one 2in (5cm) piece of fresh ginger, sliced and cut into thin strips
2 garlic cloves, finely chopped
1 bunch of scallions, cut into 2in (5cm) lengths
1 red bell pepper, seeded and sliced into thin strips
1 head broccoli, about 10oz (300g), cut into florets
1 bunch of thin asparagus, trimmed and halved crosswise
1 tbsp granulated sugar
salt and freshly ground black pepper
handful of mint leaves

METHOD

1 Heat the oil in a wok over medium-high heat, and swirl to coat the surface. Add the chilis, ginger, and garlic, and toss for a few seconds, then add the scallions. Stir-fry for 3–5 minutes, until shiny.

2 Now add the bell pepper and stir-fry for a few minutes. Add the broccoli, and stir-fry for a few minutes more, before adding the asparagus. Continue stir-frying for another minute or two until all the vegetables are crisp-tender.

3 Sprinkle in the sugar and season well with salt and pepper. Stir-fry for a few seconds until the sugar has dissolved. Remove from the heat and stir in the mint leaves. Serve immediately.

GOOD WITH Hot, fluffy rice.

4 servings

prep 15 mins • cook 15 mins

healthy option

wok

Grilled lamb cutlets and eggplant with red cabbage slaw

A range of cooked and raw vegetables provides an array of flavors to complement the simplicity of the lamb.

INGREDIENTS

1 eggplant, about 10oz (300g), thinly sliced lengthwise
salt, for sprinkling
12 lamb cutlets, trimmed of any fat
2 tbsp olive oil
salt and freshly ground black pepper

For the red cabbage slaw

1/2 small red cabbage
3 1/2oz (100g) green beans, trimmed, blanched, and thinly sliced diagonally
1 small cucumber, thinly sliced lengthwise
1 scallion, thinly sliced diagonally
1 small red onion, thinly sliced into rounds
2 celery ribs, peeled and thinly sliced diagonally
1/2 cup hazelnuts, chopped
2 tbsp extra-virgin olive oil
1 tsp balsamic vinegar

METHOD

1 Put the eggplant slices in a colander and sprinkle with salt. Allow to drain for 20 minutes, rinse, and pat dry with paper towels.

2 Heat the ridged cast-iron grill pan until hot. Brush the lamb cutlets with olive oil, and season with salt and pepper. Grill the lamb over medium heat for 3–5 minutes on each side, or until cooked to your liking. Transfer to a plate, cover with foil, and leave to rest in a warm place for 10 minutes. Meanwhile, grill the eggplant over high heat for 3 minutes on each side, until golden. Transfer to a plate, and keep warm.

3 To make the slaw, finely slice or shred the red cabbage. Put the cabbage in a bowl, and add the remaining salad ingredients. Season with salt and pepper, toss gently, and serve with the lamb cutlets and grilled eggplant.

4 servings

prep 15 mins • cook 10 mins

ridged cast-iron grill pan

Tuna with warm cucumber and fennel salad

Tuna is often cooked with Asian flavors, but here the profile is Mediterranean.

INGREDIENTS

4 tuna steaks, about $5\frac{1}{2}$oz (150g) each
6 tbsp olive oil
salt and freshly ground black pepper
1 fennel bulb, cored and sliced
1 cucumber, peeled, seeded, and diced
2 shallots, finely chopped
2 lemons (1 juiced, 1 cut into wedges)
3 tbsp chopped mint, parsley, and/or chervil
8 anchovy fillets

METHOD

1 Brush 2 tbsp of the oil over the tuna steaks. Season with salt and a generous amount of pepper. Refrigerate until ready to cook.

2 Heat 2 tbsp of the remaining oil in a frying pan over medium-high heat. Add the fennel and cook, stirring often, about 4 minutes, just until crisp-tender. Transfer to a bowl and let cool.

3 Add the cucumber, shallots, lemon juice, remaining 2 tbsp oil, and the herbs to the fennel and mix. Season with salt and pepper.

4 Heat a large frying pan over high heat until very hot. Add the tuna and cook, turning once, about 1 minute per side, until seared.

5 Transfer each tuna steak to a dinner plate. Using a slotted spoon, serve the salad on top, and drape 2 anchovies over each serving. Garnish each with a lemon wedge. Spoon the dressing around the tuna and serve immediately.

GOOD WITH Buttered new potatoes with parsley.

Tomato and harissa tart

Harissa gives this tart a fiery kick.

INGREDIENTS

one 15oz (425g) box frozen puff pastry sheets, thawed as package directs
all-purpose flour
2 tbsp red pepper or sun-dried tomato pesto
6 tomatoes, halved
2–3 tbsp harissa sauce, to taste
1 tbsp olive oil
a few sprigs of thyme, leaves picked

METHOD

1 Preheat the oven to 400°F (200°C). On a lightly floured work surface, place 1 sheet of puff pastry on top of the other, aligning the edges. Roll out the pastry into a single sheet, to a thickness of about 3/8in (1cm), and lay it on a baking sheet. Using a sharp knife, score a line about 2in (5cm) in from the edge all the way around to form a border, but do not cut all the way through the pastry. Next, using the edge of the knife, score the pastry all the way around the outer edges. This helps it to puff when cooking.

2 Working inside the border, smother the pastry with the pesto. Arrange the tomatoes on top, cut-side up. Mix the harissa with the olive oil, and drizzle over the tomatoes. Scatter the thyme leaves over the top.

3 Bake for about 15 minutes until the pastry is cooked and golden. Serve hot.

Chinese-style steamed bass

An impressive restaurant-style dish that brings out the clean, delicate flavors of the fish and is easy to prepare.

INGREDIENTS

½ cup soy sauce
½ cup Chinese rice wine or dry sherry
4 tbsp peeled and finely shredded fresh ginger
4 small sea bass, cleaned
2 tbsp Asian sesame oil
1 tsp salt
8 scallions, cut into 3in (7.5cm) shreds
one 2in (5cm) piece fresh ginger, peeled and julienned
4 garlic cloves, chopped
2 small fresh hot red chilis, seeded and minced
grated zest of 2 limes
½ cup vegetable oil

METHOD

1 Add water to the bottom compartment of a steamer and bring to a boil over high heat. Mix the soy sauce, rice wine, and shredded ginger together.

2 Score the fish with cuts about 1in (2.5cm) and ¼in (6mm) deep on both sides. Rub the fish inside and out with the sesame oil and salt.

3 Scatter one-third of the scallions in a heat-proof serving dish and add 2 fish and half of the soy sauce mixture. Place in one tier of the steamer. Repeat with another serving dish, one-third of the scallions, and the remaining fish and soy sauce mixture. Cover the steamer and cook for 10–12 minutes, until the fish is opaque when pierced with a knife.

4 Meanwhile, heat the oil in a saucepan over medium-high heat until shimmering. Sprinkle the fish with remaining scallions, julienned ginger, garlic, chilis, and lime zest. Drizzle the hot oil over the fish and serve.

4 servings

prep 15 mins • cook 10–12 mins

2-tier steamer or large pan with 2 bamboo steamers and stand

Pork chops with blue cheese stuffing

This filling is both savory and sweet and the pecans add a delightful crunchy texture.

INGREDIENTS

For the stuffing

1 sweet apple such as Golden Delicious, peeled and finely diced
3oz (85g) Roquefort or Stilton, crumbled
1/3 cup chopped pecans
2 scallions, chopped

4 center-cut pork loin chops
1 tbsp olive oil
salt and freshly ground black pepper

METHOD

1 Combine the stuffing ingredients and set aside.

2 Trim the excess fat from the pork chops. With a small sharp knife, make a horizontal slit through the fat side of each chop, cutting through the meat almost to the bone to make a pocket.

3 Divide the stuffing evenly among the chops, tucking it firmly into the pockets. Secure with wooden toothpicks.

4 Preheat the broiler. Place the pork chops on a baking sheet, brush with oil, and season with salt and pepper. Broil for 6–8 minutes on each side, depending on thickness, or until golden brown and the juices run clear. Remove the toothpicks and serve.

GOOD WITH Trimmed green beans and new potatoes.

Filet mignons with walnut pesto

A great dish for the fall, when walnuts are at their peak.

INGREDIENTS

For the walnut pesto

1 cup walnut halves
½ cup freshly grated Parmesan
2 garlic cloves, minced
2 tbsp chopped tarragon
2 tbsp chopped parsley
1½ tsp red wine vinegar
½ cup extra-virgin olive oil
salt and freshly ground black pepper

6 filet mignons, about 6oz (175g) each
olive oil, for brushing

METHOD

1 To make the walnut pesto, toast the walnuts in a 350°F (170°C) oven for 10 minutes. Let cool. Transfer to a food processor and add the Parmesan, garlic, tarragon, parsley, and vinegar. With the machine running, add the oil to make a coarse paste. Season with salt and pepper.

2 Heat a ridged frying pan over high heat. Lightly brush the steaks with oil and season with salt and pepper. Cook the steaks in the pan for about 3 minutes on each side for medium-rare. Transfer to dinner plates and serve hot, with a dollop of the walnut pesto.

GOOD WITH Roasted sweet potato wedges.

Pan-fried ham with pineapple salsa

Ham is so quick to cook, and this sweet and sour salsa makes the most of its rich flavor.

INGREDIENTS

1 tbsp olive oil
4 ham steaks
one 8oz (225g) can pineapple slices, drained and juice reserved
1 tbsp honey
1 tbsp butter
3 tomatoes, peeled and chopped
½ red onion, finely diced

METHOD

1 Heat the oil in a large nonstick frying pan over high heat. Add the ham, and cook for 3–4 minutes on each side, depending on thickness, until golden and warmed through. Remove from the pan, and set aside to keep warm.

2 Coat the pineapple slices in the honey. Melt the butter in the same frying pan. Add the pineapple, and cook for a couple of minutes, turning once, until golden and lightly charred. Remove from the pan, cool slightly, and chop into small pieces.

3 To make the salsa, combine the pineapple, tomato, and red onion in a bowl, and toss gently to mix.

4 To serve, pour the reserved pineapple juice into the same pan used for cooking the pineapple, and cook over high heat until hot. Pour over the warm ham steaks, and serve with the salsa on the side.

GOOD WITH Thick French fries.

Steak au poivre

This restaurant classic can easily be made at home.

INGREDIENTS

4 sirloin steaks or filet mignons, about 8oz (225g) each
1/2 tsp dry mustard
1–2 tsp black peppercorns
2 tbsp vegetable oil
1/4 cup sherry or brandy
2/3 cup crème fraîche

METHOD

1 Trim any excess fat from the steaks. If using filet mignons, flatten slightly with a meat mallet. Sprinkle with the mustard.

2 Crush the peppercorns in a mortar or under a saucepan and press on both sides of the steaks.

3 Heat the oil in a large frying pan over high heat. Add the steaks and cook, 2–3 minutes each side for a rare steak, 4 minutes each side for medium, and 5–6 minutes each side for well done. Transfer to a platter and tent with aluminum foil.

4 Add the sherry to the pan and stir up the browned pieces. Add the crème fraîche and cook for 3 minutes, until slightly thickened. Place the steaks on individual plates and top with the sauce. Serve hot.

GOOD WITH French fries and grilled tomatoes.

4 servings

prep 10 mins
• cook 12 mins

Sweet and sour stir-fried fish with ginger

Crispy coated fish and a flavorful, tangy sauce are perfect partners.

INGREDIENTS

1–2 tbsp cornstarch
$1^{1}/_{2}$lb (675g) thick-cut skinless white fish fillets, cut into strips
1–2 tbsp vegetable or sunflower oil
1 onion, coarsely chopped
2 garlic cloves, finely chopped
one 1in (2.5cm) piece of fresh ginger, finely grated
large handful of snow peas or sugar snap peas, sliced into strips
salt and freshly ground black pepper

For the sweet and sour sauce

2 tbsp pineapple juice
1 tbsp white wine vinegar
1 tbsp tomato purée
1 tbsp granulated sugar
2 tsp soy sauce
1 tsp cornstarch

METHOD

1 First, make the sauce by whisking together the pineapple juice, vinegar, tomato purée, sugar, soy sauce, and 1 tsp cornstarch. Set aside.

2 Put 1–2 tbsp cornstarch on a plate, and season with salt and pepper. Toss the fish in this seasoned mixture to coat.

3 In a wok, heat about half of the oil until hot, then add the fish. Stir-fry for about 5 minutes, until golden. Remove with a slotted spoon and set aside to keep warm. Carefully wipe out the wok with paper towels, and add a little more oil. When hot, add the onion and stir-fry until it begins to soften, then add the garlic and ginger and stir-fry for a few minutes longer.

4 Pour in the sweet and sour sauce and let simmer for a few minutes, stirring constantly. Reduce the heat to medium, add the peas, and stir-fry for 1 minute. Return the fish to the wok, quickly toss together to combine, and serve hot.

GOOD WITH Hot, fluffy rice.

PREPARE AHEAD The sauce can be made 1 day ahead, covered, and kept chilled until ready to use. Cook the fish just before serving, however, or the coating will become soft.

4 servings

prep 10 mins • cook 20 mins

healthy option

wok

Egg and fennel potato salad

This satisfying salad works best when the potatoes and eggs are still warm.

INGREDIENTS

4 eggs
9oz (250g) new potatoes, scrubbed
drizzle of olive oil
salt and freshly ground black pepper
1 fennel bulb, trimmed and finely chopped
handful of parsley, finely chopped
handful of dill, finely chopped (optional)

METHOD

1 Put the potatoes in a saucepan and cover with boiling water. Lightly salt the water, then cook over medium heat for 15–20 minutes, or until soft. Drain well.

2 While the potatoes are cooking, place the eggs in a saucepan and cover with water. Bring to a boil, then simmer for 10 minutes, or until hard-boiled (see page 16). Drain, and place the pan under cool running water to stop the eggs from cooking further.

3 Place the potatoes in a serving bowl, drizzle over some olive oil while they are still hot, and season with salt and pepper. Mix in the fennel, parsley, and dill (if using).

4 Drain the eggs, then peel and quarter them. Add to the potato salad, and serve immediately.

4 servings

prep 10 mins
• cook 20 mins

Pasta with mushroom sauce

Good-quality mushrooms will make this indulgent dish extra tasty.

INGREDIENTS

4 tbsp olive oil
8oz (225g) mushrooms, finely chopped
4½oz (125g) small whole mushrooms
4½oz (125g) wild mushrooms, sliced
½ cup dry white wine
3 garlic cloves, finely chopped
salt and freshly ground black pepper
handful of parsley, finely chopped
pinch of mild paprika
1 cup heavy whipping cream
12oz (350g) dried pappardelle or dried tagliatelle

METHOD

1 Gently heat the oil in a large frying pan, add all the mushrooms, and cook over low heat for 5 minutes, until they begin to release their juices. Add the wine, raise the heat, and allow to bubble for a couple of minutes. Add the garlic and lots of pepper.

2 Reduce the heat, stir in the parsley and paprika, then pour in the cream and cook, stirring occasionally, over low heat for 5 minutes.

3 Meanwhile, cook the pasta according to the package directions, or until *al dente*. Drain, reserving a small amount of the cooking water. Return the pasta to the pot and toss together with the reserved cooking water. Taste the sauce and season if needed, then toss with the pasta and serve.

4 servings

prep 10 mins
• cook 20 mins

Cauliflower gratin

A great comfort-food dish that works well as a vegetarian main course.

INGREDIENTS

1 head of cauliflower, outer leaves removed, broken into large florets
1 cup fresh bread crumbs

For the cheese sauce

3 tbsp butter
3 tbsp all-purpose flour
1½ tsp dry mustard
1¾ cups whole milk
1 cup grated sharp Cheddar cheese
salt and freshly ground black pepper

METHOD

1 Bring a large saucepan of lightly salted water to a boil. Add the cauliflower and boil for 7 minutes, or until almost tender. Drain, rinse under cold water, and drain well. Arrange the cauliflower in an oven-proof serving dish. Position the broiler rack about 8in (20cm) from the source of heat and preheat.

2 To make the cheese sauce, melt the butter in a medium saucepan over low heat. Whisk in the flour and mustard and cook without browning for 2 minutes. Remove from the heat and stir in the milk. Return to the heat and bring to a boil over medium heat, stirring often. Reduce the heat to low and simmer until thickened and no flour taste remains—about 2 minutes. Remove the pan from the heat, add ¾ cup of the Cheddar cheese, and stir until melted. Season with salt and pepper. Pour over the cauliflower.

3 Toss the remaining cheese with the bread crumbs. Sprinkle over the cauliflower. Place the dish under the broiler for 3–5 minutes, or until the sauce bubbles and the crumbs are golden. Serve hot from the dish.

GOOD WITH Any roast meat or grilled sausages.

4–6 servings

prep 15 mins
• cook 15 mins

Caramelized pork tenderloin with pecans and apricots

Pork works very well with sweet, fruity flavors—the dash of whiskey is a delightful twist.

INGREDIENTS

1–2 tsp brown sugar
1½lb (675g) pork tenderloin (in one piece)
1 tbsp olive oil
1 tbsp butter
handful of pecan halves and pieces
handful of dried apricots, halved
splash of whiskey (optional)
1 cup heavy whipping cream

METHOD

1 Rub the brown sugar all over the pork, then slice the pork crosswise into thick medallions.

2 Melt the butter in the oil in a frying pan over medium-high heat. Brown the pork for 6–8 minutes, turning once, until golden on the outside and no longer pink inside. Add the pecans and apricots, and cook for a few more minutes.

3 Increase the heat to high and add the whiskey. Let simmer for a couple of minutes until the smell of alcohol has disappeared. Reduce the heat to medium, stir in the cream, and let simmer for a few minutes longer. Serve hot.

GOOD WITH Creamy mashed potatoes.

Hamburgers

These burgers are enriched with onions and egg yolk.

INGREDIENTS

1lb (450g) ground chuck or sirloin
½ onion, minced
1 large egg yolk
salt and freshly ground black pepper
olive oil
4 sesame seed buns, cut in half and lightly toasted

METHOD

1 Combine the ground beef, onion, and egg yolk in a mixing bowl. Season generously with salt and pepper, and mix well with wet hands.

2 Shape into 4 burgers about 4in (10cm) in diameter.

3 Position a broiler rack about 6in (15cm) from the source of heat. Preheat the broiler and lightly oil the broiler pan. Add the burgers and broil for 3 minutes on each side for medium-rare, or longer if you prefer.

4 Serve burgers warm in toasted sesame seed buns.

GOOD WITH Your favorite condiments (ketchup, mustard, and mayonnaise) and toppings (sliced onions, sliced tomatoes, shredded lettuce, and dill pickles).

PREPARE AHEAD You can make the burgers 1 day in advance. Wrap them tightly in plastic wrap and chill until ready to cook.

4 servings

prep 15 mins
• cook 10 mins

freeze uncooked hamburgers for up to 3 months

Seared duck with five-spice and noodles

Tender, pan-fried duck with fragrant five-spice, orange, and cilantro.

INGREDIENTS

4 boneless duck breasts, about 5½oz (150g) each, skin on and scored in a crisscross pattern
2 tsp Chinese five-spice powder
1 tbsp butter
one 9oz (250g) package thick or medium dried udon noodles
2 tbsp fresh orange juice
1 tsp light or dark brown sugar
handful of cilantro leaves, finely chopped

METHOD

1 Rub the duck breasts all over with the five-spice powder. Melt the butter in a frying pan over high heat. Add the duck breasts, skin-side down, and cook for about 10 minutes, until the skin is golden and crisp. Carefully pour away the fat from the pan, then turn the breasts over and cook on the other side for 8 minutes. Meanwhile, cook the noodles according to the package directions, and drain well.

2 Remove the duck from the pan, and let stand for 3 minutes. Cut into diagonal slices, and arrange on a warm plate. Pour away any remaining fat, then add the orange juice to the pan along with the sugar. Let simmer for a minute or two, scraping up any pieces from the bottom of the pan with a wooden spoon.

3 Add the drained noodles and toss them in the sauce for a couple of minutes to coat. Remove from the heat, and stir in the cilantro. Serve immediately with the warm duck breasts.

4 servings

prep 10 mins • cook 20 mins

Turkey burgers

This is a sensible choice if you want a healthier alternative to a beef burger.

INGREDIENTS

1½lb (675g) ground turkey
handful of thyme leaves, chopped
grated zest and juice of 1 lemon
1 fresh red jalapeño chili pepper, seeded and finely chopped
1 tbsp butter, melted and cooled slightly
2 tbsp all-purpose flour, for dusting
olive oil or vegetable oil for frying
salt and freshly ground black pepper

To serve

4 hamburger or other bread buns
crisp iceberg lettuce leaves
tomato slices
good-quality mayonnaise

METHOD

1 Combine the turkey, thyme, lemon zest and juice, and jalapeño in a bowl. Season well with salt and pepper. Mix together until well blended.

2 Add the melted butter and, using your hands, work the mixture until it is cohesive. Divide the mixture into four, then scoop up each portion and form into a ball. Press gently with your hands to form a patty. Dust with the flour, then refrigerate for 5–10 minutes, or until firm.

3 Heat a little oil in a nonstick frying pan over medium-high heat. Fry the burgers for about 4 minutes on each side, or until golden on the outside and no longer pink inside. Serve in a bun with crisp lettuce, tomato slices, and a dollop of mayonnaise.

PREPARE AHEAD You can make the burgers 1 day in advance. Wrap them tightly in plastic wrap and chill until needed.

4 servings

prep 15 mins
• cook 15 mins

Pork scallops with bread crumb and parsley crust

Flattening meat helps it to cook quickly and evenly; this is also a good technique to try with chicken, turkey, and veal.

INGREDIENTS

$^2/_3$ cup bread crumbs, toasted
handful of parsley, chopped
2 boneless center-cut pork chops, 6–8oz (175–225g) each
1–2 eggs, beaten
1–2 tbsp all-purpose flour
1–2 tbsp olive oil
$^1/_2$ cup dry white wine
salt and freshly ground black pepper

METHOD

1 In a bowl, mix together the bread crumbs and parsley, and season well with salt and pepper. Halve each piece of pork, then sandwich each one between two sheets of plastic wrap. Pound firmly with a meat mallet or the side of a rolling pin until paper-thin. Season well with salt and pepper.

2 Put the egg(s), flour, and bread crumbs each on separate plates. Coat each piece of pork first in the flour, then the egg, and finally the bread crumbs. Heat half of the oil in a large nonstick frying pan over high heat. Add 2 of the pork scallops, and cook for 2–4 minutes on each side until golden on the outside and no longer pink inside. Remove from the pan, drain on paper towels, and set aside to keep warm while you cook the 2 remaining scallops. Keep warm while making the sauce.

3 Pour the wine into the same pan, and scrape up all the crispy pieces from the bottom with a wooden spoon. Let simmer until the smell of alcohol has disappeared, then drizzle over the pork. Serve immediately.

GOOD WITH A spinach and tomato salad, or arugula drizzled with a little lemon juice.

Thai-style minced pork with noodles

Low in fat, this tasty and speedy stir-fry is perfect for a family meal.

INGREDIENTS

1 tbsp vegetable oil
1½lb (675g) ground pork
4 garlic cloves, finely grated
pinch of salt
2 fresh hot red chili peppers, finely chopped
juice of 1 lime
splash of Asian fish sauce
splash of soy sauce
handful of cilantro, finely chopped
medium rice noodles or rice, to serve

METHOD

1 Heat the oil in a wok or large frying pan over a medium-high heat. Add the pork, garlic, and salt. Cook, stirring and tossing, until the pork is no longer pink.

2 Add the chilis, lime juice, fish sauce, and soy sauce, and stir-fry for 5 minutes longer.

3 Just before serving, stir in the cilantro. Serve hot with noodles or rice.

4 servings

prep 10 mins • cook 15 mins

healthy option

Hot and sour beef stir-fry with green beans

A tangy and spicy Chinese-style dish.

INGREDIENTS

For the hot and sour sauce

2 garlic cloves, finely grated
1 tsp dark brown sugar
6 anchovy fillets, drained and chopped
3 red jalapeño chili peppers, seeded and finely chopped
splash of Chinese rice wine
juice of 1 lime

1 tbsp honey
splash of Asian fish sauce
$1^1/_2$lb (675g) boneless sirloin (rump) steak, sliced into thin strips
handful of small green beans, trimmed
1 tbsp Asian sesame oil

METHOD

1 First, make the hot and sour sauce. Using a mortar and pestle, pound all the ingredients, except for the rice wine and lime juice, into a smooth paste. Then add the lime juice a little at a time, tasting as you go, and season with salt. Set aside.

2 In a bowl, mix together the honey and fish sauce. Add the steak strips, stirring to coat. Blanch the beans in a pan of boiling water for a few minutes, then drain and refresh in cold water.

3 Heat the oil in a wok or large frying pan over medium-high heat. Add the steak and stir-fry, tossing the meat constantly, for 3–5 minutes until it is nicely browned. Remove with a slotted spoon, and set aside.

4 Add the hot and sour sauce to the wok, and stir for a couple of minutes. Return the meat to the pan, and stir in the beans. Increase the heat to high, add the rice wine, and let bubble for a minute or two. Serve immediately with noodles or rice.

4 servings

prep 10 mins • cook 20 mins

healthy option

mortar and pestle

QUICK DESSERTS

Zabaglione

This warm Italian dessert was invented by mistake in the 1600s when fortified wine was poured into egg custard.

INGREDIENTS

4 large egg yolks
1/4 cup sugar
8 tbsp Marsala
grated zest of 1 orange
8 Italian ladyfingers (savoiardi) or biscotti, to serve

METHOD

1 Bring a large saucepan of water to a boil, then lower the heat to simmer.

2 Whisk the yolks, sugar, and Marsala with half the orange zest in a large heat-proof bowl. Place over (but not in) the simmering water. Using a balloon whisk, whisk constantly for 5–10 minutes, or until the zabaglione is pale, thick, fluffy, and warm.

3 Immediately divide the zabaglione among 4 glasses. Garnish with the remaining orange zest; serve immediately with ladyfingers or biscotti.

Eton mess

A favorite British dessert, named after Eton College, the famous English boarding school.

INGREDIENTS

12oz (350g) strawberries, hulled and sliced
2 tbsp sugar
2 tbsp orange juice or orange-flavored liqueur
1¼ cups heavy cream
5oz (140g) store-bought meringue cookies

METHOD

1 Combine the strawberries, sugar, and orange juice in a bowl, and crush them with a fork.

2 Whip the cream just until stiff peaks form. Coarsely crush the meringues into small, bite-sized pieces—you should have about 2 cups of crushed meringues.

3 Stir the crushed meringue into the whipped cream. Add the berries and their juices, and fold together. Spoon into dessert cups and serve immediately.

GOOD WITH Fresh raspberries and/or blueberries scattered over the top.

PREPARE AHEAD The berries and whipped cream can be prepared several hours in advance. Assemble just before serving.

4 servings
prep 10 mins

Baked figs with cinnamon and honey

A simple-to-prepare, but stylish end to a meal.

INGREDIENTS
6 firm figs
2 tbsp honey
2 tbsp brandy or rum
pinch of ground cinnamon

METHOD

1 Preheat the oven to 350°F (180°C). Cut the figs in half and place closely together in a shallow baking dish.

2 Drizzle with the honey and brandy, and sprinkle each fig with a generous pinch of cinnamon.

3 Bake for 20 minutes, or until softened. Check the figs after 10 minutes, since they may differ in ripeness slightly and require different cooking times. Serve warm or at room temperature.

GOOD WITH Mascarpone, vanilla ice cream, or crème fraîche.

Warm fruit compote

A good winter dessert when fresh fruit supplies are limited.

INGREDIENTS

2 tbsp butter
6 pitted dried plums, chopped
6 dried apricots, chopped
2 large apples, peeled, cored, and chopped
1 firm ripe pear, peeled, cored, and chopped
1 cinnamon stick
2 tsp sugar
2 tsp lemon juice
yogurt or honey, to serve

METHOD

1 Melt the butter in a heavy saucepan over medium heat. Add the fruit and cinnamon stick. Cook gently, stirring often, until the fruit has completely softened.

2 Stir in the sugar and heat for a couple of minutes, or until the sugar has dissolved.

3 Remove the pan from the heat, and stir in the lemon juice. Serve warm with a spoonful of yogurt or a drizzle of honey.

PREPARE AHEAD The compote can be made several days in advance, cooled, covered, and refrigerated.

4 servings

prep 10 mins
• cook 5–10 mins

Berries with citrus syrup

Juicy seasonal berries are made even more luscious with a sweet lemon-orange syrup.

INGREDIENTS

1lb (450g) mixed red berries, such as raspberries, strawberries, and red currants
$\frac{2}{3}$ cup sugar
zest of 1 lemon, cut into thin strips
1 tbsp fresh orange juice
4 sprigs mint, leaves only

METHOD

1 Place the mixed berries in a serving dish.

2 Bring the sugar and $\frac{1}{2}$ cup water to a boil in a saucepan over medium heat, stirring until the sugar dissolves. Increase the heat to high and boil for 5 minutes, until slightly reduced. Let cool. Stir in the lemon zest and orange juice.

3 Pour the syrup over the berries, and sprinkle with the mint leaves. Let stand for at least 10 minutes. Transfer to dessert glasses and serve.

GOOD WITH Whipped cream or ice cream.

PREPARE AHEAD The berries can be soaked for up to 1 hour.

healthy option

Honey-baked apricots with mascarpone

This Italian dessert, with just a hint of spice, makes the most of the short apricot season.

INGREDIENTS

4 ripe, juicy apricots, halved and pitted
3 tbsp honey
3 tbsp sliced almonds
pinch of ground ginger or cinnamon
2/3 cup mascarpone cheese, for serving

METHOD

1 Preheat the oven to 400°F (200°C). Lightly butter a shallow baking dish just large enough to hold the apricots.

2 Arrange the apricots in the dish, cut sides up. Brush with the honey, then sprinkle with the almonds and a dusting of the ginger.

3 Bake for 15 minutes, or until the apricots are tender when pierced with the tip of a knife and the almonds are toasted. Serve hot or cooled in dessert glasses, with a dollop of the mascarpone.

GOOD WITH Vanilla ice cream or thick whipped cream, instead of the mascarpone.

PREPARE AHEAD The dish can be assembled, ready for baking, several hours in advance.

4 servings

prep 10 mins
• cook 10 mins

Mango and papaya salad

Tropical fruit flavors combine in this refreshing dessert.

INGREDIENTS

one 1in (2.5cm) piece ginger in syrup, cut into thin strips
2 tbsp syrup from ginger
2 tbsp sugar
grated zest of 1 lime
2 tbsp fresh lime juice
1 pomegranate, seeds only
1 large ripe mango
1 large ripe papaya
1 small melon, such as Ogen or Charentais
lime wedges, to serve

METHOD

1 Combine the ginger, ginger syrup, sugar, and ½ cup of water in a saucepan. Bring to a boil over medium heat, stirring to dissolve the sugar. Simmer for 5–6 minutes until slightly reduced. Remove from the heat, stir in the lime zest and juice and the pomegranate seeds. Let cool.

2 Peel the mangoes. Use a sharp knife to cut the flesh away from the pits. Slice the mango and arrange the slices on a plate. Halve, seed, and peel the papaya. Cut into wedges and arrange on the mango. Halve and seed the melon. Cut the melon flesh into bite-sized chunks. Add to the mango and papaya.

3 Spoon the ginger dressing over the fruit. Serve with lime wedges.

GOOD WITH Greek yogurt or whipped cream.

PREPARE AHEAD The ginger dressing can be refrigerated for up to 2 days. The fruit can be refrigerated in an airtight container for up to 1 day.

4 servings

prep 15 mins
• cook 10 mins

healthy option

Pineapple flambé

Fresh pineapple is flamed with rum to produce this delicious, show-stopping dessert.

INGREDIENTS

1 ripe pineapple
¼ cup dark rum or brandy
2 tbsp fresh lime juice
¼ cup butter
¼ cup light brown sugar
ground cinnamon, for dusting

METHOD

1 Peel the pineapple and remove the "eyes." Slice into rounds about ½in (1cm) thick, reserving any pineapple juice. Cut out the core using a small round cookie cutter or the tip of a sharp knife.

2 Place the pineapple and its juices, rum, and lime juice in a large frying pan and cook over a medium-low heat for about 1 minute, just until the liquid is warm. Carefully ignite the pan juices with a long, wooden grill match. Cook until the flames die down.

3 Dot the pineapple with the butter and sprinkle with the brown sugar. Cook while gently shaking the pan until the butter and sugar combine into a glaze. Spoon into dessert dishes and serve hot, dusted with the cinnamon.

GOOD WITH Ice cream or whipped cream.

4 servings

prep 15–20 mins • cook 10 mins

Citrus fruit salad

Refreshing, colorful, and full of vitamins—this is sunshine in a bowl.

INGREDIENTS

3 oranges
1 grapefruit
1 ruby grapefruit
2 clementines or mandarins
juice of 1 lime
1–2 tbsp sugar (optional)
lime zest, to decorate (optional)

METHOD

1 With a sharp knife, cut away the skin and pith from the oranges and grapefruit. Cutting toward the core of the fruit, cut away each segment, sliding the knife blade close to the membrane that separates them (see page 18).

2 Place all the segments in a bowl. Squeeze any remaining juice from the membranes, then discard the membranes.

3 Peel the clementines and divide into segments. Add to the bowl, then add the lime juice. Sprinkle with the sugar, if using. Cover and refrigerate several hours, until ready to serve.

4 Using a slotted spoon, spoon the salad into dessert cups and garnish with the lime zest, if using. Serve chilled.

PREPARE AHEAD The salad can be covered and refrigerated for up to 24 hours.

Pear gratin

A sophisticated, simple, and foolproof dessert

INGREDIENTS

4 ripe Comice pears
5½oz (150g) blackberries
½ cup coarsely chopped walnuts
1 cup mascarpone cheese
2 tbsp dark brown sugar

METHOD

1 Position a broiler rack 6in (15cm) from the source of heat and preheat the broiler. Quarter the pears and remove the cores. Place skin-side down in a flame-proof serving dish. Sprinkle with the blackberries and walnuts. Drop spoonfuls of mascarpone cheese over the pears and sprinkle with the brown sugar.

2 Broil for 3–5 minutes, or until the mascarpone is bubbly and the sugar begins to caramelize. Serve warm.

GOOD WITH Crisp buttery cookies.

4 servings

prep 10 mins
• cook 3–5 mins

Strawberry yogurt mousse

This speedy dessert is bound to be a favorite with the kids.

INGREDIENTS

1lb (450g) ripe strawberries
3/4 cup evaporated milk, well chilled
2 tbsp superfine sugar
1 cup thick, Greek-style yogurt, plus more to serve

METHOD

1 Slice the strawberries and set a few aside. Divide half the strawberries among 4 dessert glasses. Purée the remaining strawberries in a food processor or blender. Push through a strainer to remove the seeds. If you do not have a food processor, mash the strawberries with a fork before pushing through a strainer.

2 Beat the chilled evaporated milk with an electric mixer on high speed for about 7 minutes, or until doubled in volume. Beat in the sugar. Stir in the strawberry purée and yogurt until well combined. Spoon into the glasses and refrigerate for 15–20 minutes, until lightly set.

3 Garnish with a dollop of yogurt and the reserved strawberries.

PREPARE AHEAD The mousse can be made several hours in advance.

4 servings

prep 15 mins, plus chilling

electric mixer

refrigerate the evaporated milk overnight or freeze for 30 minutes

Pear and grape salad

You don't often think of adding cucumber to sweet dishes, but it works perfectly in this exotic fruit salad.

INGREDIENTS

1 cucumber
2 lemon grass stalks
1/3 cup granulated or raw sugar
2 ripe red-skinned pears
1 cup green seedless grapes
1 cup red seedless grapes
1/4 cup packed small mint leaves

METHOD

1 Trim the ends from the cucumber. Cut in half lengthwise. Using a teaspoon, scoop out and discard the seeds, and slice thinly. Cut the bottom 4in (10cm) from each lemon grass stalk and discard the tops. Discard the tough outer leaves from the lemon grass. Halve the lemon grass lengthwise and smash with a rolling pin.

2 Bring the lemon grass, sugar, and a scant 1 cup of water to a boil in a saucepan over medium heat, stirring to dissolve the sugar. Boil for 1 minute. Remove from the heat and stir in the cucumber. Let cool.

3 Discard the lemon grass. Quarter and core the pears, and slice into thin wedges. Transfer to a serving bowl and add the green and red grapes, cucumber, and syrup. Refrigerate until ready to serve. Sprinkle with the mint leaves and serve chilled.

GOOD WITH Plain yogurt or Greek yogurt.

PREPARE AHEAD The salad can be refrigerated up to 2 days in advance.

Chocolate-dipped fruits

This decadent treat is perfect with after-dinner drinks.

INGREDIENTS

12 Cape gooseberries
12 strawberries
3½oz (100g) high-quality bittersweet chocolate

METHOD

1 Pull back the papery leaves of each gooseberry to expose the round orange fruit. Leave the stems and hulls on the strawberries. Line a baking sheet with wax paper.

2 Chop the chocolate. Transfer to a heat-proof bowl. Place over a saucepan of barely simmering water and melt, stirring occasionally. Remove the chocolate from the saucepan.

3 Holding the fruit by the stalks, dip each fruit into the chocolate and place on the tray. Work quickly, since the chocolate does not take long to set.

4 Refrigerate until the chocolate is set. Serve chilled.

PREPARE AHEAD The dipped fruits can be refrigerated for up to 24 hours.

4–6 servings

prep 20 mins, plus chilling • cook 10 mins

Knickerbocker glory

A truly glorious sundae, with chocolate and strawberry ice cream, peaches, and strawberry topping.

INGREDIENTS

2 peaches
8 small scoops strawberry ice cream
8 tbsp strawberry ice cream topping
4 small scoops chocolate ice cream
5fl oz (150ml) heavy cream, whipped
colored decorating sprinkles, for garnish
4 maraschino cherries, for serving
8 rolled wafer cookies, for serving

METHOD

1 Place the peaches in a saucepan of boiling water for about 30 seconds, or until the skins loosen. Drain and rinse under cold running water. Peel, pit, and slice the peaches. Divide half of the peach slices among 4 tall ice cream glasses. Top each with a scoop of strawberry ice cream and 1 tbsp of strawberry ice cream topping.

2 Repeat with the remaining strawberry ice cream, then the remaining peaches, and remaining topping. Top each with a scoop of chocolate ice cream.

3 Top each with whipped cream, a scattering of sprinkles, and a maraschino cherry. Serve immediately, with the cookies.

Banoffee pie

Always a hit, this dessert's name derives from its delicious filling of fresh bananas and toffee sauce.

INGREDIENTS

8in (20cm) baked pie or tart shell
1 cup ready-made thick caramel sauce or dulce de leche
2–3 ripe bananas
$1\frac{1}{4}$ cups heavy whipping cream
scant 1oz (25g) semisweet chocolate

METHOD

1 Place the pie shell on a serving plate. Spoon in the caramel sauce and spread evenly over the bottom. Slice the bananas and scatter over the top.

2 Put the cream in a bowl and beat with an electric mixer until soft peaks form, then spoon over the bananas. Grate the chocolate, sprinkle evenly over the top, and serve.

INDEX

Page numbers in *italics* indicate illustrations.

ACKNOWLEDGMENTS

DORLING KINDERSLEY WOULD LIKE TO THANK THE FOLLOWING:

Photographers
Carole Tuff, Tony Cambio, William Shaw, Stuart West, David Munns, David Murray, Adrian Heapy, Nigel Gibson, Kieran Watson, Roddy Paine, Gavin Sawyer, Ian O'Leary, Steve Baxter, Martin Brigdale, Francesco Guillamet, Jeff Kauck, William Reavell, and Jon Whitaker

Picture Researcher
Emma Shepherd

Proofreader
Anna Osborn

Indexer
Susan Bosanko

Useful information

Refrigerator and freezer storage guidelines

FOOD	REFRIGERATOR	FREEZER
Raw poultry, fish, and meat (small pieces)	2–3 days	3 months
Raw ground beef and poultry	1–3 days	3 months
Cooked whole roasts or whole poultry	2–3 days	9 months
Cooked poultry pieces	2–3 days	3 months
Soups and stocks	2–3 days	3–6 months
Stews	2–3 days	3 months
Pies	2–3 days	3–6 months

Oven temperature equivalents

FAHRENHEIT	CELSIUS	DESCRIPTION
225°F	110°C	Cool
250°F	130°C	Cool
275°F	140°C	Very low
300°F	150°C	Very low
325°F	160°C	Low
350°F	180°C	Moderate
375°F	190°C	Moderately hot
400°F	200°C	Hot
425°F	220°C	Hot
450°F	230°C	Very hot
475°F	240°C	Very hot